Selected Material from

Essentials of
Corporate Finance

Fifth Edition

Stephen A. Ross
Massachusetts Institute of Technology

Randolph W. Westerfield
University of Southern California

Bradford D. Jordan
University of Kentucky

with additional material from

Student Problem Manual
for use with
Essentials of Corporate Finance
Fifth Edition

Stephen A. Ross

Randolph W. Westerfield

Bradford D. Jordan

Prepared by

Thomas. H. Eyssell
University of Missouri-St. Louis

 **Learning Solutions**

Boston   Burr Ridge, IL   Dubuque, IA   New York   San Francisco   St. Louis
Bangkok   Bogotá   Caracas   Lisbon   London   Madrid
Mexico City   Milan   New Delhi   Seoul   Singapore   Sydney   Taipei   Toronto

Selected Material from
Essentials of Corporate Finance
Fifth Edition

This book is a McGraw-Hill Learning Solutions textbook and contains select material from the following sources: *Essentials of Corporate Finance*, Fifth Edition by Stephen A. Ross, Randolph W. Westerfield and Bradford D. Jordan. Copyright © 2007, 2004, 2001, 1999, by The McGraw-Hill Companies, Inc.
Student Problem Manual for use with Essentials of Corporate Finance, Fifth Edition by Stephen A. Ross, Randolph W. Westerfield and Bradford D. Jordan, prepared by Thomas H. Eyssell. Copyright © 2007, 2004, 2001, 1999, 1996 by The McGraw-Hill Companies, Inc. Reprinted with permission of the publisher. Many custom published texts are modified versions or adaptations of our best-selling textbooks. Some adaptations are printed in black and white to keep prices at a minimum, while others are in color.

2 3 4 5 6 7 8 9 0 QSR BLA 0 9 8

ISBN 13: 978-0-697-77412-5
ISBN 10: 0-697-77412-0

Editor: Ann Hayes
Production Editor: Susan Culbertson
Printer/Binder: Quebcor World
           Perfect Printing

Contents

Essentials of
CORPORATE FINANCE
FIFTH EDITION

On December 2, 1982, General Motors Acceptance Corporation (GMAC), a subsidiary of General Motors, offered some securities for sale to the public. Under the terms of the deal, GMAC promised to repay the owner of one of these securities $10,000 on December 1, 2012, but investors would receive nothing until then. Investors paid GMAC $500 for each of these securities, so they gave up $500 on December 2, 1982, for the promise of a $10,000 payment 30 years later. Such a security, for which you pay some amount today in exchange for a promised lump sum to be received at a future date, is about the simplest possible type.

Introduction to Valuation: The Time Value of Money

4

THERE ARE THREE ESSENTIAL THINGS YOU SHOULD LEARN FROM THIS CHAPTER:

- How to determine the future value of an investment made today.

- How to determine the present value of cash to be received at a future date.

- How to find the return on an investment.

Is giving up $500 in exchange for $10,000 in 30 years a good deal? On the plus side, you get back $20 for every $1 you put up. That probably sounds good, but, on the downside, you have to wait 30 years to get it. What you need to know is how to analyze this trade-off; this chapter gives you the tools you need.

Specifically, our goal here is to introduce you to one of the most important principles in finance, the time value of money. What you will learn is how to determine the value today of some cash flow to be received later. This is a very basic business skill, and it underlies the analysis of many different types of investments and financing arrangements. In fact, almost all business activities, whether they originate in marketing, management, operations, or strategy, involve comparing outlays made today to benefits projected for the future. How to do this comparison is something everyone needs to understand; this chapter gets you started.

One of the basic problems faced by the financial manager is how to determine the value today of cash flows expected in the future. For example, the jackpot in a PowerBall™ lottery drawing was $110 million. Does this mean the winning ticket was worth $110 million? The answer is no because the jackpot was actually going to pay out over a 20-year period at a rate of $5.5 million per year. How much was the ticket worth then? The answer depends on the time value of money, the subject of this chapter.

In the most general sense, the phrase *time value of money* refers to the fact that a dollar in hand today is worth more than a dollar promised at some time in the future. On a practical level, one reason for this is that you could earn interest while you waited; so, a dollar today would grow to more than a dollar later. The trade-off between money now and money later thus depends on, among other things, the rate you can earn by investing. Our goal in this chapter is to explicitly evaluate this trade-off between dollars today and dollars at some future time.

A thorough understanding of the material in this chapter is critical to understanding material in subsequent chapters, so you should study it with particular care. We will present a number of examples in this chapter. In many problems, your answer may differ from ours slightly. This can happen because of rounding and is not a cause for concern.

FUTURE VALUE AND COMPOUNDING | 4.1

The first thing we will study is future value. **Future value (FV)** refers to the amount of money an investment will grow to over some period of time at some given interest rate. Put another way, future value is the cash value of an investment at some time in the future. We start out by considering the simplest case, a single-period investment.

future value (FV)
The amount an investment is worth after one or more periods.

Investing for a Single Period

Suppose you were to invest $100 in a savings account that pays 10 percent interest per year. How much would you have in one year? You would have $110. This $110 is equal to your original *principal* of $100 plus $10 in interest that you earn. We say that $110 is the future value of $100 invested for one year at 10 percent, and we simply mean that $100 today is worth $110 in one year, given that 10 percent is the interest rate.

In general, if you invest for one period at an interest rate of r, your investment will grow to $(1 + r)$ per dollar invested. In our example, r is 10 percent, so your investment grows to $1 + .10 = 1.1$ dollars per dollar invested. You invested $100 in this case, so you ended up with $100 \times 1.10 = $110.

Investing for More Than One Period

Going back to our $100 investment, what will you have after two years, assuming the interest rate doesn't change? If you leave the entire $110 in the bank, you will earn $110 \times .10 = $11 in interest during the second year, so you will have a total of $110 + 11 = $121. This $121 is the future value of $100 in two years at 10 percent. Another way of looking at it is that one year from now you are effectively investing $110 at 10 percent for a year. This is a single-period problem, so you'll end up with $1.1 for every dollar invested, or $110 \times 1.1 = $121 total.

This $121 has four parts. The first part is the $100 original principal. The second part is the $10 in interest you earn in the first year, and the third part is another $10 you earn in the second year, for a total of $120. The last $1 you end up with (the fourth part) is interest you earn in the second year on the interest paid in the first year: $10 \times .10 = $1.

This process of leaving your money and any accumulated interest in an investment for more than one period, thereby reinvesting the interest, is called **compounding**. Compounding the interest means earning **interest on interest**, so we call the result **compound interest**. With **simple interest**, the interest is not reinvested, so interest is earned each period only on the original principal.

EXAMPLE **4.1** | **Interest on Interest**

Suppose you locate a two-year investment that pays 14 percent per year. If you invest $325, how much will you have at the end of the two years? How much of this is simple interest? How much is compound interest?

At the end of the first year, you will have $325 × (1 + .14) = $370.50. If you reinvest this entire amount, and thereby compound the interest, you will have $370.50 × 1.14 = $422.37 at the end of the second year. The total interest you earn is thus $422.37 − 325 = $97.37. Your $325 original principal earns $325 × .14 = $45.50 in interest each year, for a two-year total of $91 in simple interest. The remaining $97.37 − 91 = $6.37 results from compounding. You can check this by noting that the interest earned in the first year is $45.50. The interest on interest earned in the second year thus amounts to $45.50 × .14 = $6.37, as we calculated.

---

compounding

The process of accumulating interest in an investment over time to earn more interest.

interest on interest

Interest earned on the reinvestment of previous interest payments.

compound interest

Interest earned on both the initial principal and the interest reinvested from prior periods.

simple interest

Interest earned only on the original principal amount invested.

We now take a closer look at how we calculated the $121 future value. We multiplied $110 by 1.1 to get $121. The $110, however, was $100 also multiplied by 1.1. In other words:

$$
\begin{aligned}
\$121 &= \$110 \times 1.1 \\
&= (\$100 \times 1.1) \times 1.1 \\
&= \$100 \times (1.1 \times 1.1) \\
&= \$100 \times 1.1^2 \\
&= \$100 \times 1.21
\end{aligned}
$$

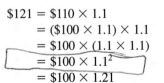

At the risk of belaboring the obvious, let's ask: How much would our $100 grow to after three years? Once again, in two years, we'll be investing $121 for one period at 10 percent. We'll end up with $1.1 for every dollar we invest, or $121 × 1.1 = $133.1 total. This $133.1 is thus:

$$
\begin{aligned}
\$133.1 &= \$121 \times 1.1 \\
&= (\$110 \times 1.1) \times 1.1 \\
&= (\$100 \times 1.1) \times 1.1 \times 1.1 \\
&= \$100 \times (1.1 \times 1.1 \times 1.1) \\
&= \$100 \times 1.1^3 \\
&= \$100 \times 1.331
\end{aligned}
$$

You're probably noticing a pattern to these calculations, so we can now go ahead and state the general result. As our examples suggest, the future value of $1 invested for t periods at a rate of r per period is:

Future value $= \$1 \times (1 + r)^t$ **[4.1]**

The expression $(1 + r)^t$ is sometimes called the *future value interest factor* (or just *future value factor*) for $1 invested at r percent for t periods and can be abbreviated as $FVIF(r, t)$.

Year	Beginning Amount	Interest Earned	Ending Amount
1	$100.00	$10.00	$110.00
2	110.00	11.00	121.00
3	121.00	12.10	133.10
4	133.10	13.31	146.41
5	146.41	14.64	161.05
		Total interest $61.05	

TABLE 4.1

Future value of $100 at 10 percent

In our example, what would your $100 be worth after five years? We can first compute the relevant future value factor as:

$$(1 + r)^t = (1 + .10)^5 = 1.1^5 = 1.6105$$

Your $100 will thus grow to:

$$\$100 \times 1.6105 = \$161.05$$

The growth of your $100 each year is illustrated in Table 4.1. As shown, the interest earned in each year is equal to the beginning amount multiplied by the interest rate of 10 percent.

In Table 4.1, notice that the total interest you earn is $61.05. Over the five-year span of this investment, the simple interest is $100 × .10 = $10 per year, so you accumulate $50 this way. The other $11.05 is from compounding.

Figure 4.1 illustrates the growth of the compound interest in Table 4.1. Notice how the simple interest is constant each year, but the compound interest you earn gets bigger every year. The size of the compound interest keeps increasing because more and more interest builds up and there is thus more to compound.

Future values depend critically on the assumed interest rate, particularly for long-lived investments. Figure 4.2 illustrates this relationship by plotting the growth of $1 for different rates and lengths of time. Notice that the future value of $1 after 10 years is about $6.20 at a 20 percent rate, but it is only about $2.60 at 10 percent. In this case, doubling the interest rate more than doubles the future value.

To solve future value problems, we need to come up with the relevant future value factors. There are several different ways of doing this. In our example, we could have multiplied 1.1 by itself five times. This would work just fine, but it would get to be very tedious for, say, a 30-year investment.

Fortunately, there are several easier ways to get future value factors. Most calculators have a key labeled "y^x." You can usually just enter 1.1, press this key, enter 5, and press the "=" key to get the answer. This is an easy way to calculate future value factors because it's quick and accurate.

Alternatively, you can use a table that contains future value factors for some common interest rates and time periods. Table 4.2 contains some of these factors. Table A.1 in Appendix A at the end of the book contains a much larger set. To use the table, find the column that corresponds to 10 percent. Then look down the rows until you come to five periods. You should find the factor that we calculated, 1.6105.

Tables such as Table 4.2 are not as common as they once were because they predate inexpensive calculators and are only available for a relatively small number of rates. Interest rates are often quoted to three or four decimal places, so the tables needed to deal with these accurately would be quite large. As a result, the "real world" has moved away from using them. We will emphasize the use of a calculator in this chapter.

A brief introduction to key financial concepts is available at **www.teachmefinance.com.**

FIGURE 4.1

Future value, simple interest, and compound interest

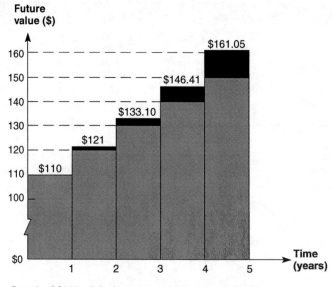

Growth of $100 original amount at 10% per year. Purple shaded area represents the portion of the total that results from compounding of interest.

FIGURE 4.2

Future value of $1 for different periods and rates

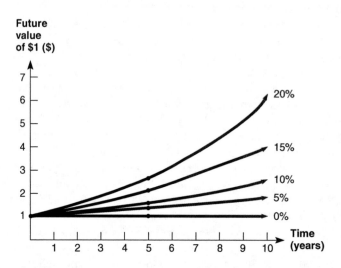

TABLE 4.2

Future value interest factors

Number of Periods	Interest Rates			
	5%	10%	15%	20%
1	1.0500	1.1000	1.1500	1.2000
2	1.1025	1.2100	1.3225	1.4400
3	1.1576	1.3310	1.5209	1.7280
4	1.2155	1.4641	1.7490	2.0736
5	1.2763	1.6105	2.0114	2.4883

These tables still serve a useful purpose. To make sure you are doing the calculations correctly, pick a factor from the table and then calculate it yourself to see that you get the same answer. There are plenty of numbers to choose from.

Compound Interest EXAMPLE 4.2

You've located an investment that pays 12 percent. That rate sounds good to you, so you invest $400. How much will you have in three years? How much will you have in seven years? At the end of seven years, how much interest have you earned? How much of that interest results from compounding?

Based on our discussion, we can calculate the future value factor for 12 percent and three years as:

$(1 + r)^t = 1.12^3 = 1.4049$

Your $400 thus grows to:

$400 \times 1.4049 = $561.97

After seven years, you will have:

$400 \times 1.12^7 = $400 \times 2.2107 = $884.27

Thus, you will more than double your money over seven years.

Since you invested $400, the interest in the $884.27 future value is $884.27 − 400 = $484.27. At 12 percent, your $400 investment earns $400 × .12 = $48 in simple interest every year. Over seven years, the simple interest thus totals 7 × $48 = $336. The other $484.27 − 336 = $148.27 is from compounding.

The effect of compounding is not great over short time periods, but it really starts to add up as the horizon grows. To take an extreme case, suppose one of your more frugal ancestors had invested $5 for you at a 6 percent interest rate 200 years ago. How much would you have today? The future value factor is a substantial $1.06^{200} = 115,125.90$ (you won't find this one in a table), so you would have $5 × 115,125.90 = $575,629.50 today. Notice that the simple interest is just $5 × .06 = $.30 per year. After 200 years, this amounts to $60. The rest is from reinvesting. Such is the power of compound interest!

How much do you need at retirement? Check out the "Money/Retirement" link at **www.about.com.**

How Much for That Island? EXAMPLE 4.3

To further illustrate the effect of compounding for long horizons, consider the case of Peter Minuit and the Indians. In 1626, Minuit bought all of Manhattan Island for about $24 in goods and trinkets. This sounds cheap, but the Indians may have gotten the better end of the deal. To see why, suppose the Indians had sold the goods and invested the $24 at 10 percent. How much would it be worth today?

Roughly 380 years have passed since the transaction. At 10 percent, $24 will grow by quite a bit over that time. How much? The future value factor is approximately:

$(1 + r)^t = 1.1^{380} \approx 5,000,000,000,000,000$

That is, 5 followed by 15 zeroes. The future value is thus on the order of $24 × 5 quadrillion, or about $120 *quadrillion* (give or take a few hundreds of trillions).

Well, $120 quadrillion is a lot of money. How much? If you had it, you could buy the United States. All of it. Cash. With money left over to buy Canada, Mexico, and the rest of the world, for that matter.

This example is something of an exaggeration, of course. In 1626, it would not have been easy to locate an investment that would pay 10 percent every year without fail for the next 380 years.

CALCULATOR HINTS

Using a Financial Calculator

Although there are the various ways of calculating future values we have described so far, many of you will decide that a financial calculator is the way to go. If you are planning on using one, you should read this extended hint; otherwise, skip it.

A financial calculator is simply an ordinary calculator with a few extra features. In particular, it knows some of the most commonly used financial formulas, so it can directly compute things like future values.

Financial calculators have the advantage that they handle a lot of the computation, but that is really all. In other words, you still have to understand the problem; the calculator just does some of the arithmetic. In fact, there is an old joke (somewhat modified) that goes like this: Anyone can make a mistake on a time value of money problem, but to really screw one up takes a financial calculator! We therefore have two goals for this section. First, we'll discuss how to compute future values. After that, we'll show you how to avoid the most common mistakes people make when they start using financial calculators.

How to Calculate Future Values with a Financial Calculator   Examining a typical financial calculator, you will find five keys of particular interest. They usually look like this:

N	**I/Y**	**PMT**	**PV**	**FV**

For now, we need to focus on four of these. The keys labeled **PV** and **FV** are just what you would guess: present value and future value. The key labeled **N** refers to the *number* of periods, which is what we have been calling *t*. Finally, **I/Y** stands for the *interest rate, which* we have called *r*.[1]

If we have the financial calculator set up right (see our next section), then calculating a future value is very simple. Take a look back at our question involving the future value of $100 at 10 percent for five years. We have seen that the answer is $161.05. The exact keystrokes will differ depending on what type of calculator you use, but here is basically all you do:

1.   Enter −100. Press the **PV** key. (The negative sign is explained below.)
2.   Enter 10. Press the **I/Y** key. (Notice that we entered 10, not .10; see below.)
3.   Enter 5. Press the **N** key.

Now we have entered all of the relevant information. To solve for the future value, we need to ask the calculator what the FV is. Depending on your calculator, you either press the button labeled "CPT" (for compute) and then press **FV** , or else you just press **FV** . Either way, you should get 161.05. If you don't (and you probably won't if this is the first time you have used a financial calculator!), we will offer some help in our next section.

Before we explain the kinds of problems that you are likely to run into, we want to establish a standard format for showing you how to use a financial calculator. Using the example we just looked at, in the future, we will illustrate such problems like this:

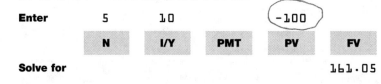

Enter	5	10		−100	
	N	**I/Y**	**PMT**	**PV**	**FV**
Solve for					161.05

CPT
↓
FV

---

[1]The reason financial calculators use N and I/Y is that the most common use for these calculators is determining loan payments. In this context, N is the number of payments and I/Y is the interest rate on the loan. But, as we will see, there are many other uses of financial calculators that don't involve loan payments and interest rates.

Here is an important tip: Appendix D in the back of the book contains some more detailed instructions for the most common types of financial calculators. See if yours is included, and, if it is, follow the instructions there if you need help. Of course, if all else fails, you can read the manual that came with the calculator.

How to Get the Wrong Answer Using a Financial Calculator There are a couple of common (and frustrating) problems that cause a lot of trouble with financial calculators. In this section, we provide some important *dos* and *don'ts*. If you just can't seem to get a problem to work out, you should refer back to this section.

There are two categories we examine: three things you need to do only once and three things you need to do every time you work a problem. The things you need to do just once deal with the following calculator settings:

1. *Make sure your calculator is set to display a large number of decimal places.* Most financial calculators only display two decimal places; this causes problems because we frequently work with numbers—like interest rates—that are very small.
2. *Make sure your calculator is set to assume only one payment per period or per year.* Some financial calculators assume monthly payments (12 per year) unless you say otherwise.
3. *Make sure your calculator is in "end" mode.* This is usually the default, but you can accidently change to "begin" mode.

If you don't know how to set these three things, see Appendix D or your calculator's operating manual. There are also three things you need to do *every time you work a problem:*

1. *Before you start, completely clear out the calculator.* This is very important. Failure to do this is the number one reason for wrong answers; you simply must get in the habit of clearing the calculator every time you start a problem. How you do this depends on the calculator (see Appendix D), but you must do more than just clear the display. For example, on a Texas Instruments BA II Plus you must press 2nd then CLR TVM for *clear time value of money.* There is a similar command on your calculator. Learn it!

    Note that turning the calculator off and back on won't do it. Most financial calculators remember everything you enter, even after you turn them off. In other words, they remember all your mistakes unless you explicitly clear them out. Also, if you are in the middle of a problem and make a mistake, *clear it out and start over.* Better to be safe than sorry.
2. *Put a negative sign on cash outflows.* Most financial calculators require you to put a negative sign on cash outflows and a positive sign on cash inflows. As a practical matter, this usually just means that you should enter the present value amount with a negative sign (because normally the present value represents the amount you give up today in exchange for cash inflows later). You enter a negative value on the BA II Plus by first entering a number and then pressing the +/− key. By the same token, when you solve for a present value, you shouldn't be surprised to see a negative sign.
3. *Enter the rate correctly.* Financial calculators assume that rates are quoted in percent, so if the rate is .08 (or 8 percent), you should enter 8, not .08.

If you follow these guidelines (especially the one about clearing out the calculator), you should have no problem using a financial calculator to work almost all of the problems in this and the next few chapters. We'll provide some additional examples and guidance where appropriate.

CONCEPT QUESTIONS

4.1a What do we mean by the future value of an investment?

4.1b What does it mean to compound interest? How does compound interest differ from simple interest?

4.1c In general, what is the future value of $1 invested at r per period for t periods?

4.2 | PRESENT VALUE AND DISCOUNTING

When we discuss future value, we are thinking of questions such as the following: What will my $2,000 investment grow to if it earns a 6.5 percent return every year for the next six years? The answer to this question is what we call the future value of $2,000 invested at 6.5 percent for six years (verify that the answer is about $2,918).

There is another type of question that comes up even more often in financial management that is obviously related to future value. Suppose you need to have $10,000 in 10 years, and you can earn 6.5 percent on your money. How much do you have to invest today to reach your goal? You can verify that the answer is $5,327.26. How do we know this? Read on.

The Single-Period Case

We've seen that the future value of $1 invested for one year at 10 percent is $1.10. We now ask a slightly different question: How much do we have to invest today at 10 percent to get $1 in one year? In other words, we know the future value here is $1, but what is the **present value (PV)**? The answer isn't too hard to figure out. Whatever we invest today will be 1.1 times bigger at the end of the year. Since we need $1 at the end of the year:

present value (PV)
The current value of future cash flows discounted at the appropriate discount rate.

Present value × 1.1 = $1

Or, solving for the present value:

Present value = $1/1.1 = $.909

discount
Calculate the present value of some future amount.

In this case, the present value is the answer to the following question: What amount, invested today, will grow to $1 in one year if the interest rate is 10 percent? Present value is thus just the reverse of future value. Instead of compounding the money forward into the future, we **discount** it back to the present.

EXAMPLE 4.4   **Single-Period PV**

Suppose you need $400 to buy textbooks next year. You can earn 7 percent on your money. How much do you have to put up today?

We need to know the PV of $400 in one year at 7 percent. Proceeding as above:

Present value × 1.07 = $400

We can now solve for the present value:

Present value = $400 × (1/1.07) = $373.83

Thus, $373.83 is the present value. Again, this just means that investing this amount for one year at 7 percent will result in your having a future value of $400.

From our examples, the present value of $1 to be received in one period is generally given as:

$$PV = \$1 \times [1/(1 + r)] = \$1/(1 + r)$$

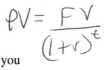

We next examine how to get the present value of an amount to be paid in two or more periods into the future.

Present Values for Multiple Periods

$$PV = \frac{FV}{(1+r)^t}$$

Suppose you need to have $1,000 in two years. If you can earn 7 percent, how much do you have to invest to make sure that you have the $1,000 when you need it? In other words, what is the present value of $1,000 in two years if the relevant rate is 7 percent?

Based on your knowledge of future values, you know that the amount invested must grow to $1,000 over the two years. In other words, it must be the case that:

$$\begin{aligned}\$1,000 &= PV \times 1.07 \times 1.07 \\ &= PV \times 1.07^2 \\ &= PV \times 1.1449\end{aligned}$$

Given this, we can solve for the present value:

Present value = $1,000/1.1449 = $873.44

Therefore, $873.44 is the amount you must invest in order to achieve your goal.

Saving Up   **EXAMPLE 4.5**

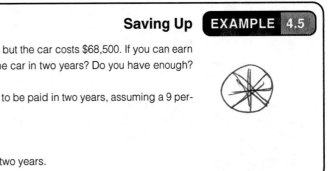

You would like to buy a new automobile. You have $50,000, but the car costs $68,500. If you can earn 9 percent, how much do you have to invest today to buy the car in two years? Do you have enough? Assume the price will stay the same.

What we need to know is the present value of $68,500 to be paid in two years, assuming a 9 percent rate. Based on our discussion, this is:

PV = $68,500/1.09² = $68,500/1.1881 = $57,655.08

You're still about $7,655 short, even if you're willing to wait two years.

As you have probably recognized by now, calculating present values is quite similar to calculating future values, and the general result looks much the same. The present value of $1 to be received t periods into the future at a discount rate of r is:

$$PV = \$1 \times [1/(1 + r)^t] = \$1/(1 + r)^t \qquad \textbf{[4.2]}$$

discount rate
The rate used to calculate the present value of future cash flows.

The quantity in brackets, $1/(1 + r)^t$, goes by several different names. Since it's used to discount a future cash flow, it is often called a *discount factor*. With this name, it is not surprising that the rate used in the calculation is often called the **discount rate**. We will tend to call it this in talking about present values. The quantity in brackets is also called the *present value interest factor* (or just *present value factor*) for $1 at r percent for t periods and is sometimes abbreviated as PVIF(r, t). Finally, calculating the present value of a future cash flow to determine its worth today is commonly called **discounted cash flow (DCF) valuation**.

discounted cash flow (DCF) valuation
Valuation calculating the present value of a future cash flow to determine its value today.

TABLE 4.3	Number of Periods	Interest Rates			
		5%	10%	15%	20%
Present value interest factors	1	.9524	.9091	.8696	.8333
	2	.9070	.8264	.7561	.6944
	3	.8638	.7513	.6575	.5787
	4	.8227	.6830	.5718	.4823
	5	.7835	.6209	.4972	.4019

To illustrate, suppose you need $1,000 in three years. You can earn 15 percent on your money. How much do you have to invest today? To find out, we have to determine the present value of $1,000 in three years at 15 percent. We do this by discounting $1,000 back three periods at 15 percent. With these numbers, the discount factor is:

$$1/(1 + .15)^3 = 1/1.5209 = .6575$$

The amount you must invest is thus:

$$\$1,000 \times .6575 = \$657.50$$

We say that $657.50 is the present, or discounted, value of $1,000 to be received in three years at 15 percent.

There are tables for present value factors just as there are tables for future value factors, and you use them in the same way (if you use them at all). Table 4.3 contains a small set of these factors. A much larger set can be found in Table A.2 in Appendix A.

In Table 4.3, the discount factor we just calculated, .6575, can be found by looking down the column labeled "15%" until you come to the third row. Of course, you could use a financial calculator, as we illustrate next.

CALCULATOR HINTS

You solve present value problems on a financial calculator just like you do future value problems. For the example we just examined (the present value of $1,000 to be received in three years at 15 percent), you would do the following:

Enter	3	15			1,000
	N	**I/Y**	**PMT**	**PV**	**FV**
Solve for				−657.50	

Notice that the answer has a negative sign; as we discussed above, that's because it represents an outflow today in exchange for the $1,000 inflow later.

EXAMPLE 4.6   **Deceptive Advertising**

Recently, some businesses have been saying things like "Come try our product. If you do, we'll give you $100 just for coming by!" If you read the fine print, what you find out is that they will give you a savings certificate that will pay you $100 in 25 years or so. If the going interest rate on such certificates is 10 percent per year, how much are they really giving you today?

(continued)

What you're actually getting is the present value of $100 to be paid in 25 years. If the discount rate is 10 percent per year, then the discount factor is:

$$1/1.1^{25} = 1/10.8347 = .0923$$

This tells you that a dollar in 25 years is worth a little more than nine cents today, assuming a 10 percent discount rate. Given this, the promotion is actually paying you about $.0923 \times \$100 = \$9.23$. Maybe this is enough to draw customers, but it's not $100.

As the length of time until payment grows, present values decline. As Example 4.6 illustrates, present values tend to become small as the time horizon grows. If you look out far enough, they will always get close to zero. Also, for a given length of time, the higher the discount rate is, the lower is the present value. Put another way, present values and discount rates are inversely related. Increasing the discount rate decreases the PV and vice versa.

The relationship between time, discount rates, and present values is illustrated in Figure 4.3. Notice that by the time we get to 10 years, the present values are all substantially smaller than the future amounts.

High r = low PV

Higher t causes PV to ↓ to 0

CONCEPT QUESTIONS

4.2a   What do we mean by the present value of an investment?

4.2b   The process of discounting a future amount back to the present is the opposite of doing what?

4.2c   What do we mean by discounted cash flow, or DCF, valuation?

4.2d   In general, what is the present value of $1 to be received in *t* periods, assuming a discount rate of *r* per period?

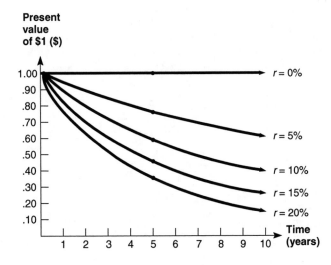

FIGURE 4.3

Present value of $1 for different periods and rates

4.3 | MORE ON PRESENT AND FUTURE VALUES

If you look back at the expressions we came up with for present and future values, you will see there is a very simple relationship between the two. We explore this relationship and some related issues in this section.

Present versus Future Value

For a downloadable, Windows-based financial calculator, go to **www.calculator.org**.

What we called the present value factor is just the reciprocal of (that is, 1 divided by) the future value factor:

> Future value factor $= (1 + r)^t$
> Present value factor $= 1/(1 + r)^t$

In fact, the easy way to calculate a present value factor on many calculators is to first calculate the future value factor and then press the **1/x** key to flip it over.

If we let FV_t stand for the future value after t periods, then the relationship between future value and present value can be written very simply as one of the following:

$$PV \times (1 + r)^t = FV_t$$
$$PV = FV_t/(1 + r)^t = FV_t \times [1/(1 + r)^t]$$

[4.3]

This last result we will call the *basic present value equation*. We will use it throughout the text. There are a number of variations that come up, but this simple equation underlies many of the most important ideas in finance.

EXAMPLE 4.7   **Evaluating Investments**

To give you an idea of how we will be using present and future values, consider the following simple investment. Your company proposes to buy an asset for $335. This investment is very safe. You will sell off the asset in three years for $400. You know you could invest the $335 elsewhere at 10 percent with very little risk. What do you think of the proposed investment?

This is not a good investment. Why not? Because you can invest the $335 elsewhere at 10 percent. If you do, after three years it will grow to:

$$\$335 \times (1 + r)^t = \$335 \times 1.1^3$$
$$= \$335 \times 1.331$$
$$= \$445.89$$

Since the proposed investment only pays out $400, it is not as good as other alternatives we have. Another way of saying the same thing is to notice that the present value of $400 in three years at 10 percent is:

$$\$400 \times [1/(1 + r)^t] = \$400/1.1^3 = \$400/1.331 = \$300.53$$

This tells us that we only have to invest about $300 to get $400 in three years, not $335. We will return to this type of analysis later on.

Determining the Discount Rate

It will turn out that we will frequently need to determine what discount rate is implicit in an investment. We can do this by looking at the basic present value equation:

$$PV = FV_t/(1 + r)^t$$

There are only four parts to this equation: the present value (PV), the future value (FV$_t$), the discount rate (r), and the life of the investment (t). Given any three of these, we can always find the fourth.

Finding *r* for a Single-Period Investment   EXAMPLE 4.8

You are considering a one-year investment. If you put up $1,250, you will get back $1,350. What rate is this investment paying?

First, in this single-period case, the answer is fairly obvious. You are getting a total of $100 in addition to your $1,250. The implicit rate on this investment is thus $100/1,250 = 8 percent.

More formally, from the basic present value equation, the present value (the amount you must put up today) is $1,250. The future value (what the present value grows to) is $1,350. The time involved is one period, so we have:

$$\$1,250 = \$1,350/(1 + r)^1$$
$$1 + r = \$1,350/1,250 = 1.08$$
$$r = 8\%$$

In this simple case, of course, there was no need to go through this calculation, but, as we describe below, it gets a little harder when there is more than one period.

To illustrate what happens with multiple periods, let's say that we are offered an investment that costs us $100 and will double our money in eight years. To compare this to other investments, we would like to know what discount rate is implicit in these numbers. This discount rate is called the *rate of return,* or sometimes just *return,* on the investment. In this case, we have a present value of $100, a future value of $200 (double our money), and an eight-year life. To calculate the return, we can write the basic present value equation as:

$$PV = FV_t/(1 + r)^t$$
$$\$100 = \$200/(1 + r)^8$$

It could also be written as:

$$(1 + r)^8 = \$200/100 = 2$$

We now need to solve for r. There are three ways we could do it:

1. Use a financial calculator. (See below.)
2. Solve the equation for $1 + r$ by taking the eighth root of both sides. Since this is the same thing as raising both sides to the power of ⅛, or .125, this is actually easy to do with the **y^x** key on a calculator. Just enter 2, then press **y^x** , enter .125, and press the **=** key. The eighth root should be about 1.09, which implies that r is 9 percent.
3. Use a future value table. The future value factor for eight years is equal to 2. If you look across the row corresponding to eight periods in Table A.1, you will see that a future value factor of 2 corresponds to the 9 percent column, again implying that the return here is 9 percent.

Actually, in this particular example, there is a useful "back of the envelope" means of solving for r—the Rule of 72. For reasonable rates of return, the time it takes to double your money is given approximately by 72/r%. In our example, this means that 72/r% = 8 years, implying that r is 9 percent as we calculated. This rule is fairly accurate for discount rates in the 5 percent to 20 percent range.

Why does the Rule of 72 work? See **www.datachimp.com.**

A Head of State's Cabinet

It used to be that trading in collectibles such as baseball cards, art, and old toys occurred mostly at auctions, swap meets, and collectible shops, all of which were limited to regional traffic. However, with the growing popularity of on-line auctions such as eBay, trading in collectibles has expanded to an international arena. The most visible form of collectible is probably the baseball card, but Furbies, Beanie Babies, and Pokémon cards have been extremely hot collectibles in the recent past. However, it's not just fad items that spark interest from collectors; virtually anything of sentimental value from days gone by is considered collectible, and, more and more, collectibles are being viewed as investments.

Collectibles typically provide no cash flows, except when sold, and condition and buyer sentiment are the major determinants of value. The rates of return have been amazing at times, but care is needed in interpreting them. For example, in December 2004, the so-called Badminton cabinet was purchased by Prince Hans-Adam II, Liechtenstein's head of state, for display in the Liechtenstein Museum in Vienna. The eighteenth-century Italian cabinet is made of ebony, gilt bronze, and stone, and is trimmed in lapis lazuli, agate, and jasper. The price for this piece of furniture? How about $36.7 million! It had previously changed hands for $15.2 million in 1990. While this looks like an extraordinary jump in value to the untrained eye, check for yourself that the actual return on the investment was about 6.05 percent per year. Plus you had the problem of dusting the 12 ½ foot tall cabinet over the years.

Another collectible that has grown in popularity recently is older Namiki nibs. These lacquered fountain pens were manufactured during the 1920s and 1930s and have been called exquisite works of art. A particularly appealing pen, which was manufactured around 1930, sold for $39,600 during a 2004 auction. The same pen was priced at about $11,400 only three years earlier. This also seems like a very high return to the untrained eye, and indeed it is! Check for yourself that the return was about 51.45 percent per year.

Stamp collecting (or philately) is a popular activity. A one-cent stamp featuring Benjamin Franklin was issued in 1851 and printed in imperforate sheets, meaning no perforations, so you had to cut them apart with scissors or a razor. You could have purchased this stamp at auction in 2004 for $7,000. Again, to the untrained eye it appears to be a whopping gain, yet the return is about 9.13 percent per year.

Looking back at these investments, the Nakimi pen had the highest return recently. The problem is that to earn this return you had to purchase the pen when it was new and store it. Looking ahead, the corresponding problem is predicting what the future value of the next hot collectible will be. You will earn a positive return only if the market value of your asset rises above the purchase price at some point in the future. That, of course, is rarely assured. For example, Barbie dolls have in the past been a popular collectible, however, most collectors say the new Barbies, which today are mass-marketed at discount stores, will probably have little or no value as collectibles at any time in the future, so we don't recommend them for your retirement investing.

The nearby *Reality Bytes* box provides some examples of rates of return on collectibles. See if you can verify the numbers reported there.

EXAMPLE 4.9 Double Your Fun

You have been offered an investment that promises to double your money every 10 years. What is the approximate rate of return on the investment?

From the Rule of 72, the rate of return is given approximately by $72/r\% = 10$, so the rate is approximately $72/10 = 7.2\%$. Verify that the exact answer is 7.177 percent.

A slightly more extreme example involves money bequeathed by Benjamin Franklin, who died on April 17, 1790. In his will, he gave 1,000 pounds sterling to Massachusetts and the city of Boston. He gave a like amount to Pennsylvania and the city of Philadelphia. The money was paid to Franklin when he held political office, but he believed that politicians should not be paid for their service (it appears that this view is not widely shared by modern-day politicians).

Franklin originally specified that the money should be paid out 100 years after his death and used to train young people. Later, however, after some legal wrangling, it was agreed that the money would be paid out in 1990, 200 years after Franklin's death. By that time, the Pennsylvania bequest had grown to about $2 million; the Massachusetts bequest had grown to $4.5 million. The money was used to fund the Franklin Institutes in Boston and Philadelphia. Assuming that 1,000 pounds sterling was equivalent to 1,000 dollars, what rate of return did the two states earn (the dollar did not become the official U.S. currency until 1792)?

For Pennsylvania, the future value is $2 million and the present value is $1,000. There are 200 years involved, so we need to solve for r in the following:

$$\$1,000 = \$2 \text{ million}/(1 + r)^{200}$$
$$(1 + r)^{200} = 2,000$$

Solving for r, we see that the Pennsylvania money grew at about 3.87 percent per year. The Massachusetts money did better; verify that the rate of return in this case was 4.3 percent. Small differences can add up!

We can illustrate how to calculate unknown rates using a financial calculator using these numbers. For Pennsylvania, you would do the following:

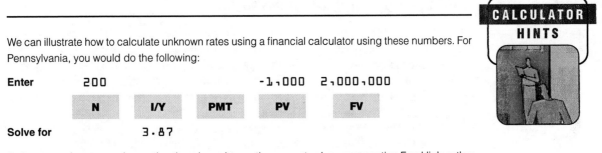

As in our previous examples, notice the minus sign on the present value, representing Franklin's outlay made many years ago. What do you change to work the problem for Massachusetts?

Saving for College EXAMPLE 4.10

You estimate that you will need about $80,000 to send your child to college in eight years. You have about $35,000 now. If you can earn 20 percent per year, will you make it? At what rate will you just reach your goal?

If you can earn 20 percent, the future value of your $35,000 in eight years will be:

FV = $35,000 × 1.20^8 = $35,000 × 4.2998 = $150,493.59

So, you will make it easily. The minimum rate is the unknown r in the following:

FV = $35,000 × $(1 + r)^8$ = $80,000
$(1 + r)^8$ = $80,000/35,000 = 2.2857

Therefore, the future value factor is 2.2857. Looking at the row in Table A.1 that corresponds to eight periods, we see that our future value factor is roughly halfway between the ones shown for 10 percent

(continued)

(2.1436) and 12 percent (2.4760), so you will just reach your goal if you earn approximately 11 percent. To get the exact answer, we could use a financial calculator or we could solve for r:

$$(1 + r)^8 = \$80,000/35,000 = 2.2857$$
$$1 + r = 2.2857^{(1/8)} = 2.2857^{.125} = 1.1089$$
$$r = 10.89\%$$

EXAMPLE 4.11

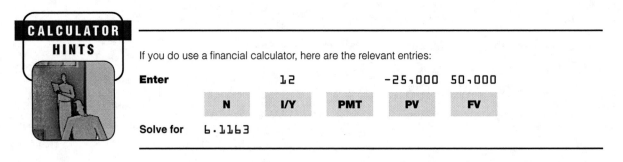

Only 18,262.5 Days to Retirement

You would like to retire in 50 years as a millionaire. If you have $10,000 today, what rate of return do you need to earn to achieve your goal?

The future value is $1,000,000. The present value is $10,000, and there are 50 years until retirement. We need to calculate the unknown discount rate in the following:

$$\$10,000 = \$1,000,000/(1 + r)^{50}$$
$$(1 + r)^{50} = 100$$

The future value factor is thus 100. You can verify that the implicit rate is about 9.65 percent.

Finding the Number of Periods

Suppose we were interested in purchasing an asset that costs $50,000. We currently have $25,000. If we can earn 12 percent on this $25,000, how long until we have the $50,000? Finding the answer involves solving for the last variable in the basic present value equation, the number of periods. You already know how to get an approximate answer to this particular problem. Notice that we need to double our money. From the Rule of 72, this will take about $72/12 = 6$ years at 12 percent.

To come up with the exact answer, we can again manipulate the basic present value equation. The present value is $25,000, and the future value is $50,000. With a 12 percent discount rate, the basic equation takes one of the following forms:

$$\$25,000 = \$50,000/1.12^t$$
$$\$50,000/25,000 = 1.12^t = 2$$

We thus have a future value factor of 2 for a 12 percent rate. We now need to solve for t. If you look down the column in Table A.1 that corresponds to 12 percent, you will see that a future value factor of 1.9738 occurs at six periods. It will thus take about six years, as we calculated. To get the exact answer, we have to explicitly solve for t (or use a financial calculator). If you do this, you will find that the answer is 6.1163 years, so our approximation was quite close in this case.

CALCULATOR HINTS

If you do use a financial calculator, here are the relevant entries:

Enter		12		-25,000	50,000
	N	**I/Y**	**PMT**	**PV**	**FV**
Solve for	6.1163				

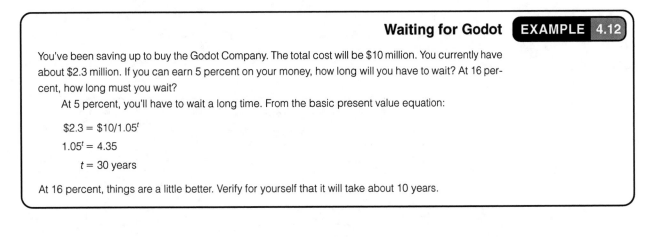

Waiting for Godot   EXAMPLE 4.12

You've been saving up to buy the Godot Company. The total cost will be $10 million. You currently have about $2.3 million. If you can earn 5 percent on your money, how long will you have to wait? At 16 percent, how long must you wait?

At 5 percent, you'll have to wait a long time. From the basic present value equation:

$2.3 = $10/1.05^t

1.05^t = 4.35

t = 30 years

At 16 percent, things are a little better. Verify for yourself that it will take about 10 years.

This example finishes our introduction to basic time value of money concepts. Table 4.4 on page 109 summarizes present value and future value calculations for future reference. As our nearby *Work the Web* box shows, online calculators are widely available to handle these calculations, but it is still important to know what is going on.

Using a Spreadsheet for Time Value of Money Calculations

SPREADSHEET STRATEGIES

More and more, businesspeople from many different areas (and not just finance and accounting) rely on spreadsheets to do all the different types of calculations that come up in the real world. As a result, in this section, we will show you how to use a spreadsheet to handle the various time value of money problems we presented in this chapter. We will use Microsoft Excel™, but the commands are similar for other types of software. We assume you are already familiar with basic spreadsheet operations.

As we have seen, you can solve for any one of the following four potential unknowns: future value, present value, the discount rate, or the number of periods. With a spreadsheet, there is a separate formula for each. In Excel, these are as follows:

Learn more about using Excel for time value and other calculations at **www.studyfinance. com.**

To Find	Enter This Formula
Future value	= FV (rate,nper,pmt,pv)
Present value	= PV (rate,nper,pmt,fv)
Discount rate	= RATE (nper,pmt,pv,fv)
Number of periods	= NPER (rate,pmt,pv,fv)

In these formulas, pv and fv are present and future value, nper is the number of periods, and rate is the discount, or interest, rate.

There are two things that are a little tricky here. First, unlike a financial calculator, the spreadsheet requires that the rate be entered as a decimal. Second, as with most financial calculators, you have to put a negative sign on either the present value or the future value to solve for the rate or the number of periods. For the same reason, if you solve for a present value, the answer will have a negative sign unless you input a negative future value. The same is true when you compute a future value.

To illustrate how you might use these formulas, we will go back to an example in the chapter. If you invest $25,000 at 12 percent per year, how long until you have $50,000? You might set up a spreadsheet like this:

	A	B	C	D	E	F	G	H
1								
2	**Using a spreadsheet for time value of money calculations**							
3								
4	If we invest $25,000 at 12 percent, how long until we have $50,000? We need to solve for the							
5	unknown number of periods, so we use the formula NPER (rate, pmt, pv, fv).							
6								
7	Present value (pv):	$25,000						
8	Future value (fv):	$50,000						
9	Rate (rate):	.12						
10								
11	Periods:	**6.116255**						
12								
13	The formula entered in cell B11 is =NPER(B9,0,-B7,B8); notice that pmt is zero and that pv has a							
14	negative sign on it. Also notice that the rate is entered as a decimal, not a percentage.							

WORK THE WEB

How important is the time value of money? A recent search on one Web engine returned over 3.2 million hits! It is important to understand the calculations behind the time value of money, but the advent of financial calculators and spreadsheets has eliminated the need for tedious calculations. In fact, many Web sites offer time value of money calculators. The following is an example from Moneychimp's Web site, www.moneychimp.com. You need $50,000 in 20 years and will invest your money at 10.2 percent. How much do you need to deposit today? To use the calculator, you simply enter the values and hit "Calculate." The results look like this:

Inputs		
Future Value:	$	50,000.00
Years:		20
Discount Rate:		10.2 %
	Calculate	
Results		
Present Value:	$	7,167.01

Who said time value of money calculations are hard?

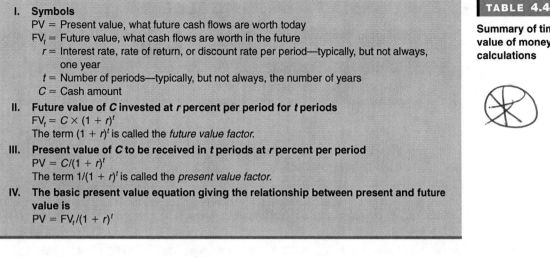

I. **Symbols**
   PV = Present value, what future cash flows are worth today
   FV_t = Future value, what cash flows are worth in the future
   r = Interest rate, rate of return, or discount rate per period—typically, but not always, one year
   t = Number of periods—typically, but not always, the number of years
   C = Cash amount

II. **Future value of C invested at r percent per period for t periods**
   $FV_t = C \times (1 + r)^t$
   The term $(1 + r)^t$ is called the *future value factor*.

III. **Present value of C to be received in t periods at r percent per period**
   $PV = C/(1 + r)^t$
   The term $1/(1 + r)^t$ is called the *present value factor*.

IV. **The basic present value equation giving the relationship between present and future value is**
   $PV = FV_t/(1 + r)^t$

TABLE 4.4

Summary of time value of money calculations

CONCEPT QUESTIONS

4.3a What is the basic present value equation?

4.3b What is the Rule of 72?

SUMMARY AND CONCLUSIONS

This chapter has introduced you to the basic principles of present value and discounted cash flow valuation. In it, we explained a number of things about the time value of money, including:

1. For a given rate of return, the value at some point in the future of an investment made today can be determined by calculating the future value of that investment.

2. The current worth of a future cash flow can be determined for a given rate of return by calculating the present value of the cash flow involved.

3. The relationship between present value and future value for a given rate r and time t is given by the basic present value equation:

$$PV = FV_t/(1 + r)^t$$

As we have shown, it is possible to find any one of the four components (PV, FV_t, r, or t) given the other three.

The principles developed in this chapter will figure prominently in the chapters to come. The reason for this is that most investments, whether they involve real assets or financial assets, can be analyzed using the discounted cash flow, or DCF, approach. As a result, the DCF approach is broadly applicable and widely used in practice. Before going on, therefore, you might want to do some of the problems below.

CHAPTER REVIEW AND SELF-TEST PROBLEMS

4.1 **Calculating Future Values.**   Assume you deposit $1,000 today in an account that pays 8 percent interest. How much will you have in four years?

4.2 **Calculating Present Values.**   Suppose you have just celebrated your 19th birthday. A rich uncle set up a trust fund for you that will pay you $100,000 when you turn 25. If the relevant discount rate is 11 percent, how much is this fund worth today?

4.3 **Calculating Rates of Return.**   You've been offered an investment that will double your money in 12 years. What rate of return are you being offered? Check your answer using the Rule of 72.

4.4 **Calculating the Number of Periods.**   You've been offered an investment that will pay you 7 percent per year. If you invest $10,000, how long until you have $20,000? How long until you have $30,000?

▪ Answers to Chapter Review and Self-Test Problems

4.1 We need to calculate the future value of $1,000 at 8 percent for four years. The future value factor is:

$$1.08^4 = 1.3605$$

The future value is thus $1,000 \times 1.3605 = \$1,360.50$.

4.2 We need the present value of $100,000 to be paid in six years at 11 percent. The discount factor is:

$$1/1.11^6 = 1/1.8704 = .5346$$

The present value is thus about $53,460.

4.3 Suppose you invest, say, $100. You will have $200 in 12 years with this investment. So, $100 is the amount you have today, the present value, and $200 is the amount you will have in 12 years, or the future value. From the basic present value equation, we have:

$$\$200 = \$100 \times (1 \times r)^{12}$$
$$2 = (1 \times r)^{12}$$

From here, we need to solve for r, the unknown rate. As shown in the chapter, there are several different ways to do this. We will take the 12th root of 2 (by raising 2 to the power of 1/12):

$$2^{(1/12)} = 1 + r$$
$$1.0595 = 1 + r$$
$$r = 5.95\%$$

Using the Rule of 72, we have $72/t = r\%$, or $72/12 = 6\%$, so our answer looks good (remember that the Rule of 72 is only an approximation).

4.4 The basic equation is:

$$\$20,000 = \$10,000 \times (1 + .07)^t$$
$$2 = (1 + .07)^t$$

If we solve for t, we get that $t = 10.24$ years. Using the Rule of 72, we get $72/7 = 10.29$ years, so, once again, our answer looks good. To get $30,000, verify for yourself that you will have to wait 16.24 years.

CRITICAL THINKING AND CONCEPTS REVIEW

4.1 **Compounding.** What is compounding? What is discounting?

4.2 **Compounding and Periods.** As you increase the length of time involved, what happens to future values? What happens to present values?

4.3 **Compounding and Interest Rates.** What happens to a future value if you increase the rate r? What happens to a present value?

4.4 **Future Values.** Suppose you deposit a large sum in an account that earns a low interest rate and simultaneously deposit a small sum in an account with a high interest rate. Which account will have the larger future value?

4.5 **Ethical Considerations.** Take a look back at Example 4.6. Is it deceptive advertising? Is it unethical to advertise a future value like this without a disclaimer?

To answer the next five questions, refer to the GMAC security we discussed to open the chapter.

4.6 **Time Value of Money.** Why would GMAC be willing to accept such a small amount today ($500) in exchange for a promise to repay 20 times that amount ($10,000) in the future?

4.7 **Call Provisions.** GMAC has the right to buy back the securities any time it wishes by paying $10,000 (this is a term of this particular deal). What impact does this feature have on the desirability of this security as an investment?

4.8 **Time Value of Money.** Would you be willing to pay $500 today in exchange for $10,000 in 30 years? What would be the key considerations in answering yes or no? Would your answer depend on who is making the promise to repay?

4.9 **Investment Comparison.** Suppose that when GMAC offered the security for $500, the U.S. Treasury had offered an essentially identical security. Do you think it would have had a higher or lower price? Why?

4.10 **Length of Investment.** The GMAC security is actively bought and sold on the New York Stock Exchange. If you looked in *The Wall Street Journal* today, do you think the price would exceed the $500 original price? Why? If you looked in the year 2009, do you think the price would be higher or lower than today's price? Why?

QUESTIONS AND PROBLEMS

Basic
(Questions 1–15)

1. **Simple Interest versus Compound Interest.** First City Bank pays 7 percent simple interest on its savings account balances, whereas Second City Bank pays 7 percent interest compounded annually. If you made a $6,000 deposit in each bank, how much more money would you earn from your Second City Bank account at the end of 10 years?

2. **Calculating Future Values.** For each of the following, compute the future value:

Present Value	Years	Interest Rate	Future Value
$ 3,150	3	18%	
7,810	10	6	
89,305	17	12	
227,382	22	5	

3. Calculating Present Values.   For each of the following, compute the present value:

Present Value	Years	Interest Rate	Future Value
	9	4%	$ 15,451
	4	12	51,557
	16	22	886,073
	21	20	550,164

 4. Calculating Interest Rates.   Solve for the unknown interest rate in each of the following:

Present Value	Years	Interest Rate	Future Value
$ 221	5		$ 307
425	7		761
25,000	18		136,771
40,200	16		255,810

5. Calculating the Number of Periods.   Solve for the unknown number of years in each of the following:

Present Value	Years	Interest Rate	Future Value
$ 250		6%	$ 1,105
1,941		5	3,860
21,320		14	387,120
32,500		29	198,212

6. Calculating Interest Rates.   Assume the total cost of a college education will be $280,000 when your child enters college in 18 years. You presently have $39,000 to invest. What annual rate of interest must you earn on your investment to cover the cost of your child's college education?

7. Calculating the Number of Periods.   At 7 percent interest, how long does it take to double your money? To quadruple it?

8. Calculating Rates of Return.   In 2004, a silver dollar minted at the Carson City mint in 1880 sold for $17,825. What was the rate of return on this investment?

9. Calculating the Number of Periods.   You're trying to save to buy a new $140,000 Ferrari. You have $30,000 today that can be invested at your bank. The bank pays 4.2 percent annual interest on its accounts. How long will it be before you have enough to buy the car?

10. Calculating Present Values.   Imprudential, Inc., has an unfunded pension liability of $800 million that must be paid in 20 years. To assess the value of the firm's stock, financial analysts want to discount this liability back to the present. If the relevant discount rate is 7 percent, what is the present value of this liability?

11. Calculating Present Values.   You have just received notification that you have won the $2 million first prize in the Centennial Lottery. However, the prize will be awarded on your 100th birthday (assuming you're around to collect), 80 years from now. What is the present value of your windfall if the appropriate discount rate is 13 percent?

12. **Calculating Future Values.**   Your coin collection contains 50 1952 silver dollars. If your grandparents purchased them for their face value when they were new, how much will your collection be worth when you retire in 2058, assuming they appreciate at a 5.3 percent annual rate?

13. **Calculating Interest Rates and Future Values.**   In 1895, the first U.S. Open Golf Championship was held. The winner's prize money was $150. In 2004, the winner's check was $1,125,000. What was the annual percentage increase in the winner's check over this period? If the winner's prize increases at the same rate, what will it be in 2040?

14. **Calculating Rates of Return.**   In 2004, a copper penny minted in 1792 was valued at $400,000. For this to have been true, what was the annual increase in the value of the penny?

15. **Calculating Rates of Return.**   Although appealing to more refined tastes, art as a collectible has not always performed so profitably. During 2003, Sotheby's sold the Edgar Degas bronze sculpture *Petite danseuse de quartorze ans* at auction for a price of $10,311,500. Unfortunately for the previous owner, he had purchased it in 1999 at a price of $12,377,500. What was his annual rate of return on this sculpture?

16. **Calculating Rates of Return.**   Referring to the GMAC security we discussed at the very beginning of the chapter:

    a.   Based on the $500 price, what rate was GMAC paying to borrow money?

    b.   Suppose that on December 1, 2005, this security's price was $6,998.79. If an investor had purchased it for $500 at the offering and sold it on this day, what annual rate of return would she have earned?

    c.   If an investor had purchased the security at market on December 1, 2005, and held it until it matured, what annual rate of return would she have earned?

17. **Calculating Present Values.**   Suppose you are still committed to owning a $140,000 Ferrari (see Question 9). If you believe your mutual fund can achieve a 10.75 percent annual rate of return, and you want to buy the car in 10 years on the day you turn 30, how much must you invest today?

18. **Calculating Future Values.**   You have just made your first $4,000 contribution to your individual retirement account. Assuming you earn a 12 percent rate of return and make no additional contributions, what will your account be worth when you retire in 45 years? What if you wait 10 years before contributing? (Does this suggest an investment strategy?)

19. **Calculating Future Values.**   You are scheduled to receive $13,000 in two years. When you receive it, you will invest it for six more years at 8 percent per year. How much will you have in eight years?

20. **Calculating the Number of Periods.**   You expect to receive $30,000 at graduation in two years. You plan on investing it at 9 percent until you have $140,000. How long will you wait from now? (Better than the situation in Question 9, but still no Ferrari.)

21. **Calculating Future Values.**   You have $9,000 to deposit. Regency Bank offers 12 percent per year compounded monthly (1 percent per month), while King Bank offers 12 percent but will only compound annually. How much will your investment be worth in 10 years at each bank?

Intermediate
(Questions 16–25)

22. **Calculating Interest Rates.**　An investment offers to triple your money in 24 months (don't believe it). What rate per six months are you being offered?

23. **Calculating the Number of Periods.**　You can earn .4 percent per month at your bank. If you deposit $1,300, how long must you wait until your account has grown to $2,500?

24. **Calculating Present Values.**　You need $50,000 in nine years. If you can earn .55 percent per month, how much will you have to deposit today?

25. **Calculating Present Values.**　You have decided that you want to be a millionaire when you retire in 45 years. If you can earn an 11 percent annual return, how much do you have to invest today? What if you can earn 5 percent?

WHAT'S ON THE WEB?

4.1　**Calculating Future Values.**　Go to www.dinkytown.net and follow the "Savings Calculator" link. If you currently have $10,000 and invest this money at 9 percent, how much will you have in 30 years? Assume you will not make any additional contributions. How much will you have if you can earn 11 percent?

4.2　**Calculating the Number of Periods.**　Go to www.dinkytown.net and follow the "Cool Million" link. You want to be a millionaire. You can earn 11.5 percent per year. Using your current age, at what age will you become a millionaire if you have $25,000 to invest, assuming you make no other deposits (ignore inflation)?

4.3　**Calculating the Number of Periods.**　Go to www.financecenter.com/consumertools and follow the "Calculators" link and find the "How much, at what rate, when?" calculator. You want to buy a Lamborghini Murciélago. Assume the price of the car is $330,000 and you have $35,000. If you can earn an 11 percent return, how long must you wait to buy this car (assuming the price stays the same)?

4.4　**Calculating Rates of Return.**　Use the FinanceCenter calculator to solve the following problem. You still want to buy the Lamborghini Murciélago, but you have $60,000 to invest and want to buy the car in 15 years. What interest rate do you have to earn to accomplish this (assuming the price stays the same)?

4.5　**Future Values and Taxes.**　Taxes can greatly affect the future value of your investment. The Financial Calculators Web site at www.fincalc.com has a financial calculator that adjusts your return for taxes. Find the "How long until my savings reach my goal?" link on this page to find this calculator. Suppose you have $50,000 to invest today. If you can earn a 12 percent return and no additional annual savings, how much will you have in 20 years? (Enter 0 percent as the tax rate.) Now, assume that your marginal tax rate is 27.5 percent. How much will you have at this tax rate?

www.mhhe.com/rwj

What do Jason Varitek, Michael Vick, and Carlos Beltran have in common? All three athletes signed big contracts at the end of 2004 or the beginning of 2005. The contract values were reported as $40 million, $119 million, and $130 million, respectively. But reported numbers are often misleading. For example, in December 2004, catcher Jason Varitek re-signed with the world champion Boston Red Sox. His contract called for a signing bonus of $4 million and a salary of $9 million per year over each of the next four years. Not bad, especially for someone who makes a living using the

5 Discounted Cash Flow Valuation

"tools of ignorance" (jock jargon for a catcher's equipment), but not as good as outfielder Beltran's deal.

A closer look at the numbers shows that both Jason and Carlos did pretty well, but nothing like the quoted figures. Using Carlos's contract as an example, the value was reported to be $119 million, but it was actually payable over several years. It consisted of a $7 million signing bonus, plus $112 million in future salary and bonuses. The remainder was to be distributed as $12 million in 2005, $14 million in 2006, $12 million in 2007, and $18.5 million per year in 2008 through 2011. Since the payments were spread out over time, we must consider the time value of money, which means his contract was worth less than reported. How much did he really get? This chapter gives you the "tools of knowledge" to answer this question.

In our previous chapter, we learned how to examine single, lump-sum future payments to determine their current, or

AFTER STUDYING THIS CHAPTER, YOU SHOULD HAVE A GOOD UNDERSTANDING OF:

- How to determine the future and present value of investments with multiple cash flows.

- How loan payments are calculated and how to find the interest rate on a loan.

- How loans are amortized or paid off.

- How interest rates are quoted (and misquoted).

present, value. This is a useful skill, but we need to go further and figure out how to handle multiple future payments because that is the much more common situation. For example, most loans (including student loans) involve receiving a lump sum today and making future payments.

More generally, most types of business decisions, including decisions concerning marketing, operations, and strategy, involve the comparison of costs incurred today with cash inflows hoped for later. Evaluating the cost-benefit trade-off requires the tools that we develop in this chapter.

Because discounted cash flow valuation is so important, students who learn this material well will find that life is much easier down the road. Getting it straight now will save you a lot of headaches later.

In our previous chapter, we covered the basics of discounted cash flow valuation. However, so far, we have only dealt with single cash flows. In reality, most investments have multiple cash flows. For example, if Sears is thinking of opening a new department store, there will be a large cash outlay in the beginning and then cash inflows for many years. In this chapter, we begin to explore how to value such investments.

When you finish this chapter, you should have some very practical skills. For example, you will know how to calculate your own car payments or student loan payments. You will also be able to determine how long it will take to pay off a credit card if you make the minimum payment each month (a practice we do not recommend). We will show you how to compare interest rates to determine which are the highest and which are the lowest, and we will also show you how interest rates can be quoted in different, and at times deceptive, ways.

5.1 | FUTURE AND PRESENT VALUES OF MULTIPLE CASH FLOWS

Thus far, we have restricted our attention to either the future value of a lump-sum present amount or the present value of some single future cash flow. In this section, we begin to study ways to value multiple cash flows. We start with future value.

Future Value with Multiple Cash Flows

Suppose you deposit $100 today in an account paying 8 percent. In one year, you will deposit another $100. How much will you have in two years? This particular problem is relatively easy. At the end of the first year, you will have $108 plus the second $100 you deposit, for a total of $208. You leave this $208 on deposit at 8 percent for another year. At the end of this second year, the account is worth:

$208 × 1.08 = $224.64

Figure 5.1 is a *time line* that illustrates the process of calculating the future value of these two $100 deposits. Figures such as this one are very useful for solving complicated problems. Anytime you are having trouble with a present or future value problem, drawing a time line will usually help you to see what is happening.

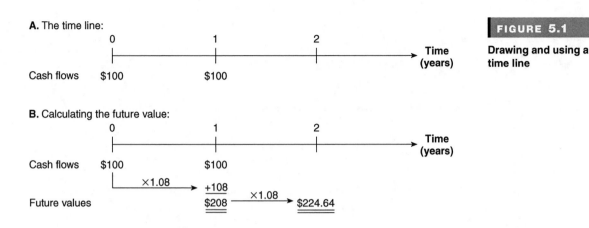

A. The time line:

B. Calculating the future value:

FIGURE 5.1

Drawing and using a
time line

In the first part of Figure 5.1, we show the cash flows on the time line. The most important thing is that we write them down where they actually occur. Here, the first cash flow occurs today, which we label as Time 0. We therefore put $100 at Time 0 on the time line. The second $100 cash flow occurs one year from today, so we write it down at the point labeled as Time 1. In the second part of Figure 5.1, we calculate the future values one period at a time to come up with the final $224.64.

Saving Up Revisited   **EXAMPLE 5.1**

You think you will be able to deposit $4,000 at the end of each of the next three years in a bank account paying 8 percent interest. You currently have $7,000 in the account. How much will you have in three years? In four years?

At the end of the first year, you will have:

$7,000 × 1.08 + 4,000 = $11,560

At the end of the second year, you will have:

$11,560 × 1.08 + 4,000 = $16,484.80

Repeating this for the third year gives:

$16,484.80 × 1.08 + 4,000 = $21,803.58

Therefore, you will have $21,803.58 in three years. If you leave this on deposit for one more year (and don't add to it), at the end of the fourth year you'll have:

$21,803.58 × 1.08 = $23,547.87

When we calculated the future value of the two $100 deposits, we simply calculated the balance as of the beginning of each year and then rolled that amount forward to the next year. We could have done it another, quicker way. The first $100 is on deposit for two years at 8 percent, so its future value is:

$100 × 1.08^2 = $100 × 1.1664 = $116.64

The second $100 is on deposit for one year at 8 percent, and its future value is thus:

$100 × 1.08 = $108.00

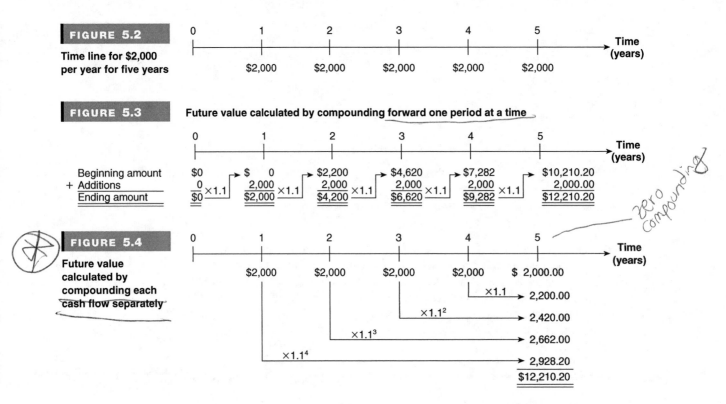

FIGURE 5.2

Time line for $2,000 per year for five years

FIGURE 5.3

FIGURE 5.4

Future value calculated by compounding each cash flow separately

The total future value, as we previously calculated, is equal to the sum of these two future values:

$$116.64 + 108 = \$224.64$$

Based on this example, there are two ways to calculate future values for multiple cash flows: (1) compound the accumulated balance forward one year at a time or (2) calculate the future value of each cash flow first and then add these up. Both give the same answer, so you can do it either way.

To illustrate the two different ways of calculating future values, consider the future value of $2,000 invested at the end of each of the next five years. The current balance is zero, and the rate is 10 percent. We first draw a time line as shown in Figure 5.2.

On the time line, notice that nothing happens until the end of the first year when we make the first $2,000 investment. This first $2,000 earns interest for the next four (not five) years. Also notice that the last $2,000 is invested at the end of the fifth year, so it earns no interest at all.

Figure 5.3 illustrates the calculations involved if we compound the investment one period at a time. As illustrated, the future value is $12,210.20.

Figure 5.4 goes through the same calculations, but it uses the second technique. Naturally, the answer is the same.

EXAMPLE 5.2   Saving Up Once Again

If you deposit $100 in one year, $200 in two years, and $300 in three years, how much will you have in three years? How much of this is interest? How much will you have in five years if you don't add additional amounts? Assume a 7 percent interest rate throughout.

(continued)

We will calculate the future value of each amount in three years. Notice that the $100 earns interest for two years, and the $200 earns interest for one year. The final $300 earns no interest. The future values are thus:

$100 × 1.07² = $114.49
$200 × 1.07 = 214.00
+$300 = $300.00

Total future value = $628.49

3 years w/3 cashflows

The future value is thus $628.49. The total interest is:

$628.49 − (100 + 200 + 300) = $28.49

How much will you have in five years? We know that you will have $628.49 in three years. If you leave that in for two more years, it will grow to:

$628.49 × 1.07² = $628.49 × 1.1449 = $719.56

Notice that we could have calculated the future value of each amount separately. Once again, be careful about the lengths of time. As we previously calculated, the first $100 earns interest for only four years, the second deposit earns three years' interest, and the last earns two years' interest:

$100 × 1.07⁴ = $100 × 1.3108 = $131.08
$200 × 1.07³ = $200 × 1.2250 = 245.01
+$300 × 1.07² = $300 × 1.1449 = 343.47

Total future value = $719.56

5 year w/3 cash flows

Present Value with Multiple Cash Flows

It will turn out that we will very often need to determine the present value of a series of future cash flows. As with future values, there are two ways we can do it. We can either discount back one period at a time, or we can just calculate the present values individually and add them up.

Suppose you need $1,000 in one year and $2,000 more in two years. If you can earn 9 percent on your money, how much do you have to put up today to exactly cover these amounts in the future? In other words, what is the present value of the two cash flows at 9 percent?

The present value of $2,000 in two years at 9 percent is:

$2,000/1.09² = $1,683.36

The present value of $1,000 in one year is:

$1,000/1.09 = $917.43

Therefore, the total present value is:

$1,683.36 + 917.43 = $2,600.79

To see why $2,600.79 is the right answer, we can check to see that after the $2,000 is paid out in two years, there is no money left. If we invest $2,600.79 for one year at 9 percent, we will have:

$2,600.79 × 1.09 = $2,834.86

We take out $1,000, leaving $1,834.86. This amount earns 9 percent for another year, leaving us with:

$1,834.86 × 1.09 = $2,000

This is just as we planned. As this example illustrates, the present value of a series of future cash flows is simply the amount that you would need today in order to exactly duplicate those future cash flows (for a given discount rate).

An alternative way of calculating present values for multiple future cash flows is to discount back to the present one period at a time. To illustrate, suppose we had an investment that was going to pay $1,000 at the end of every year for the next five years. To find the present value, we could discount each $1,000 back to the present separately and then add the results up. Figure 5.5 illustrates this approach for a 6 percent discount rate. As shown, the answer is $4,212.37 (ignoring a small rounding error).

Alternatively, we could discount the last cash flow back one period and add it to the next-to-the-last cash flow:

$1,000/1.06 + 1,000 = $943.40 + 1,000 = $1,943.40

We could then discount this amount back one period and add it to the Year 3 cash flow:

$1,943.40/1.06 + 1,000 = $1,833.40 + 1,000 = $2,833.40

This process could be repeated as necessary. Figure 5.6 illustrates this approach and the remaining calculations.

As the accompanying *Reality Bytes* box shows, calculating present values is a vital step in comparing alternative cash flows. We will have much more to say on this subject in subsequent chapters.

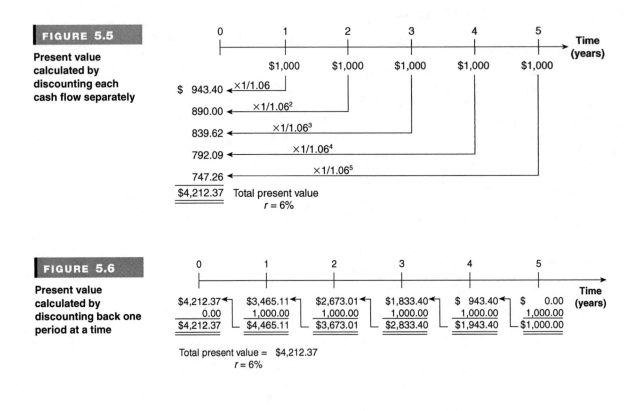

FIGURE 5.5

Present value calculated by discounting each cash flow separately

FIGURE 5.6

Present value calculated by discounting back one period at a time

REALITY | BYTES

Jackpot!

If you, or someone you know, is a regular lottery player, you probably already understand that you are 20 times more likely to be killed by a lightning bolt than to win a big lottery jackpot. How bad are the odds? Nearby you will find a table comparing your chances of winning the Mega Millions Lottery to other events.

Big Game: Is It Worth the Gamble?

Odds of winning Mega Millions jackpot	1:135,145,920*
Odds of being killed by a venomous spider	1:57,018,763
Odds of being killed by a dog bite	1:11,403,753
Odds of being killed by lightning	1:6,479,405
Odds of being killed by drowning	1:690,300
Odds of being killed falling from a bed or other furniture	1:388,411
Odds of being killed in a car crash	1:6,029

*Source: Virginia Lottery Web site. All other odds from the National Safety Council.

Sweepstakes may have different odds than lotteries, but the odds may not be much better. Probably the largest advertised grand prize ever was Pepsi's "Play for Billion," which, you guessed it, has a $1 billion (billion!) prize. Not bad for a day's work, but you still have to read the fine print. It turns out that the winner would be paid $5 million per year for the next 20 years, $10 million per year for years 21 to 39, and a lump sum $710 million in 40 years. From what you have learned, you know the value of the sweepstakes wasn't even close to $1 billion. In fact, at an interest rate of 10 percent, the present value is about $70.7 million.

Lottery jackpots are often paid out over 20 or more years, but the winner often can choose to take a lump sum cash payment instead. For some, the cash option is a lot better. In December 2004, a retired waitress in Massachusetts lost a lawsuit against the lottery in her state because they wouldn't pay out the winnings as a lump sum. She had won $5.6 million, which was to be paid out as $280,000 immediately and $280,000 per year for the next 19 years. However, since she was 94, she argued that she wouldn't be around to enjoy the money. When a lottery allows a cash option, a rule of thumb is that the cash option will be about one-half of the reported prize. Using this rule of thumb on the waitress's winnings, she would have received about $2.8 million in cash. So, what discount rate does this imply? Remembering that the first payment occurs immediately, we find the rate to be about 8.92 percent.

Some lotteries make your decision a little tougher. The Ontario Lottery will pay you either $2,000 a week for the rest of your life or $1.3 million now. (That's in Canadian dollars, by the way.) Of course, there is the chance you might die in the near future, so the lottery guarantees that your heirs will collect the $2,000 weekly payments until the 20th anniversary of the first payment, or until you would have turned 91, whichever comes first. This payout scheme complicates your decision quite a bit. If you live for only the 20-year minimum, the break-even interest rate between the two options is about 5.13 percent per year, compounded weekly. If you expect to live longer than the 20-year minimum, you might be better off accepting $2,000 per week for life. Of course, if you manage to invest the $1.3 million lump sum at a rate of return of about 8 percent per year (compounded weekly), you can have your cake and eat it too since the investment will return $2,000 at the end of each week forever! Taxes complicate the decision in this case because the lottery payments are all on an aftertax basis. Thus, the rates of return in this example would have to be aftertax as well.

How Much Is It Worth?   EXAMPLE 5.3

You are offered an investment that will pay you $200 in one year, $400 the next year, $600 the next year, and $800 at the end of the next year. You can earn 12 percent on very similar investments. What is the most you should pay for this one?

We need to calculate the present value of these cash flows at 12 percent. Taking them one at a time gives:

$$\$200 \times 1/1.12^1 = \$200/1.1200 = \$\ 178.57$$
$$\$400 \times 1/1.12^2 = \$400/1.2544 = \ 318.88$$
$$\$600 \times 1/1.12^3 = \$600/1.4049 = \ 427.07$$
$$+\$800 \times 1/1.12^4 = \$800/1.5735 = \ 508.41$$
$$\text{Total present value} = \$1,432.93$$

Sum of PVs

33

If you can earn 12 percent on your money, then you can duplicate this investment's cash flows for $1,432.93, so this is the most you should be willing to pay.

EXAMPLE 5.4

How Much Is It Worth? Part 2

You are offered an investment that will make three $5,000 payments. The first payment will occur four years from today. The second will occur in five years, and the third will follow in six years. If you can earn 11 percent, what is the most this investment is worth today? What is the future value of the cash flows?

We will answer the questions in reverse order to illustrate a point. The future value of the cash flows in six years is:

$$\$5,000 \times 1.11^2 + 5,000 \times 1.11 + 5,000 = \$6,160.50 + 5,550 + 5,000$$
$$= \$16,710.50$$

The present value must be:

$$\$16,710.50/1.11^6 = \$8,934.12$$

Let's check this. Taking them one at a time, the PVs of the cash flows are:

$$\$5,000 \times 1/1.11^6 = \$5,000/1.8704 = \$2,673.20$$
$$\$5,000 \times 1/1.11^5 = \$5,000/1.6851 = \quad 2,967.26$$
$$+\$5,000 \times 1/1.11^4 = \$5,000/1.5181 = \quad \underline{3,293.65}$$
$$\text{Total present value} = \underline{\$8,934.12}$$

This is as we previously calculated. The point we want to make is that we can calculate present and future values in any order and convert between them using whatever way seems most convenient. The answers will always be the same as long as we stick with the same discount rate and are careful to keep track of the right number of periods.

CALCULATOR HINTS

How to Calculate Present Values with Multiple Future Cash Flows Using a Financial Calculator

To calculate the present value of multiple cash flows with a financial calculator, we will simply discount the individual cash flows one at a time using the same technique we used in our previous chapter, so this is not really new. There is a shortcut, however, that we can show you. We will use the numbers in Example 5.3 to illustrate.

To begin, of course, we first remember to clear out the calculator! Next, from Example 5.3, the first cash flow is $200 to be received in one year and the discount rate is 12 percent, so we do the following:

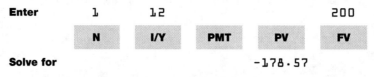

Enter	1	12			200
	N	**I/Y**	**PMT**	**PV**	**FV**
Solve for				−178.57	

Now you can write down this answer to save it, but that's inefficient. All calculators have a memory where you can store numbers. Why not just save it there? Doing so cuts way down on mistakes because you don't have to write down and/or rekey numbers, and it's much faster.

Next we value the second cash flow. We need to change N to 2 and FV to 400. As long as we haven't changed anything else, we don't have to reenter I/Y or clear out the calculator, so we have:

Enter   2   400

| N | I/Y | PMT | PV | FV |

Solve for   −318.88

You save this number by adding it to the one you saved in our first calculation, and so on for the remaining two calculations.

As we will see in a later chapter, some financial calculators will let you enter all of the future cash flows at once, but we'll discuss that subject when we get to it.

A Note on Cash Flow Timing

In working present and future value problems, cash flow timing is critically important. In almost all such calculations, it is implicitly assumed that the cash flows occur at the *end* of each period. In fact, all the formulas we have discussed, all the numbers in a standard present value or future value table, and, very importantly, all the preset (or default) settings on a financial calculator or spreadsheet assume that cash flows occur at the end of each period. Unless you are very explicitly told otherwise, you should always assume that this is what is meant.

As a quick illustration of this point, suppose you are told that a three-year investment has a first-year cash flow of $100, a second-year cash flow of $200, and a third-year cash flow of $300. You are asked to draw a time line. Without further information, you should always assume that the time line looks like this:

On our time line, notice how the first cash flow occurs at the end of the first period, the second at the end of the second period, and the third at the end of the third period.

We will close out this section by answering the question we posed concerning Carlos Beltran's contract at the beginning of the chapter. Recall that the contract called for a signing bonus of $7 million to be paid immediately, plus a salary and bonuses of $112 million, to be distributed as $12 million in 2005, $14 million in 2006, $12 million in 2007, and $18.5 million per year for 2008 through 2011. If 12 percent is the appropriate interest rate, what kind of deal did the Mets' new centerfielder catch?

To answer, we can calculate the present value by discounting each year's salary back to the present as follows (notice we assumed the future salaries will be paid at the end of the year):

Year 0: $7,000,000   = $7,000,000
Year 1: $12,000,000 × 1/1.12^1 = $10,714,285.71
Year 2: $14,000,000 × 1/1.12^2 = $11,160,714.29
Year 3: $12,000,000 × 1/1.12^3 = $8,541,362.97
              .   .   .
              .   .   .
              .   .   .
Year 7: $18,500,000 × 1/1.12^7 = $8,368,460.48

If you fill in the missing rows and then add (do it for practice), you will see that Beltran's contract had a present value of about $77.41 million, less than 2/3 of the $119 million value reported, but still pretty good. And of course, playing for the Mets, Beltran will probably have his Octobers free as well.

SPREADSHEET STRATEGIES

How to Calculate Present Values with Multiple Future Cash Flows Using a Spreadsheet

Just as we did in our previous chapter, we can set up a basic spreadsheet to calculate the present values of the individual cash flows as follows. Notice that we have simply calculated the present values one at a time and added them up.

	A	B	C	D	E	F
1						
2		Using a spreadsheet to value multiple cash flows				
3						
4	What is the present value of $200 in one year, $400 the next year, $600 the next year, and $800 the					
5	last year if the discount rate is 12 percent?					
6						
7	Rate:	.12				
8						
9	Year	Cash flows	Present values	Formula used		
10	1	$200	$178.57	=PV($B$7,A10,0,-B10)		
11	2	$400	$318.88	=PV($B$7,A11,0,-B11)		
12	3	$600	$427.07	=PV($B$7,A12,0,-B12)		
13	4	$800	$508.41	=PV($B$7,A13,0,-B13)		
14						
15		Total PV:	**$1,432.93**	=SUM(C10:C13)		
16						
17	Notice the negative signs inserted in the PV formulas. These just make the present values have					
18	positive signs. Also, the discount rate in cell B7 is entered as $B$7 (an "absolute" reference) because					
19	it is used over and over. We could have just entered ".12" instead, but our approach is more flexible.					
20						
21						
22						

CONCEPT QUESTIONS

5.1a   Describe how to calculate the future value of a series of cash flows.

5.1b   Describe how to calculate the present value of a series of cash flows.

5.1c   Unless we are explicitly told otherwise, what do we always assume about the timing of cash flows in present and future value problems?

5.2 | VALUING LEVEL CASH FLOWS: ANNUITIES AND PERPETUITIES

We will frequently encounter situations where we have multiple cash flows that are all the same amount. For example, a very common type of loan repayment plan calls for the borrower to repay the loan by making a series of equal payments for some length of time.

Almost all consumer loans (such as car loans) and home mortgages feature equal payments, usually made each month.

More generally, a series of constant, or level, cash flows that occur at the end of each period for some fixed number of periods is called an ordinary **annuity**; or, more correctly, the cash flows are said to be in ordinary annuity form. Annuities appear very frequently in financial arrangements, and there are some useful shortcuts for determining their values. We consider these next.

annuity
A level stream of cash flows for a fixed period of time.

Present Value for Annuity Cash Flows

Suppose we were examining an asset that promised to pay $500 at the end of each of the next three years. The cash flows from this asset are in the form of a three-year, $500 ordinary annuity. If we wanted to earn 10 percent on our money, how much would we offer for this annuity?

From the previous section, we know that we can discount each of these $500 payments back to the present at 10 percent to determine the total present value:

$$
\begin{aligned}
\text{Present value} &= \$500/1.1^1 + 500/1.1^2 + 500/1.1^3 \\
&= \$500/1.10 + 500/1.21 + 500/1.331 \\
&= \$454.55 + 413.22 + 375.66 \\
&= \$1,243.43
\end{aligned}
$$

This approach works just fine. However, we will often encounter situations where the number of cash flows is quite large. For example, a typical home mortgage calls for monthly payments over 30 years, for a total of 360 payments. If we were trying to determine the present value of those payments, it would be useful to have a shortcut.

Since the cash flows on an annuity are all the same, we can come up with a very useful variation on the basic present value equation. It turns out that the present value of an annuity of C dollars per period for t periods when the rate of return, or interest rate, is r is given by:

$$
\begin{aligned}
\text{Annuity present value} &= C \times \left(\frac{1 - \text{Present value factor}}{r} \right) \\
&= C \times \left\{ \frac{1 - [1/(1 + r)^t]}{r} \right\}
\end{aligned}
$$

[5.1]

The term in parentheses on the first line is sometimes called the present value interest factor for annuities and abbreviated PVIFA(r, t).

The expression for the annuity present value may look a little complicated, but it isn't difficult to use. Notice that the term in square brackets on the second line, $1/(1 + r)^t$, is the same present value factor we've been calculating. In our example just above, the interest rate is 10 percent and there are three years involved. The usual present value factor is thus:

$$\text{Present value factor} = 1/1.1^3 = 1/1.331 = .75131$$

To calculate the annuity present value factor, we just plug this in:

$$
\begin{aligned}
\text{Annuity present value factor} &= (1 - \text{Present value factor})/r \\
&= (1 - .75131)/.10 \\
&= .248685/.10 = 2.48685
\end{aligned}
$$

Just as we calculated before, the present value of our $500 annuity is then:

$$\text{Annuity present value} = \$500 \times 2.48685 = \$1,243.43$$

TABLE 5.1	Interest Rates			
Number of Periods	5%	10%	15%	20%
1	.9524	.9091	.8696	.8333
2	1.8594	1.7355	1.6257	1.5278
3	2.7232	2.4869	2.2832	2.1065
4	3.5460	3.1699	2.8550	2.5887
5	4.3295	3.7908	3.3522	2.9906

Annuity present value interest factors

EXAMPLE 5.5

How Much Can You Afford?

After carefully going over your budget, you have determined you can afford to pay $632 per month toward a new sports car. You call up your local bank and find out that the going rate is 1 percent per month for 48 months. How much can you borrow?

To determine how much you can borrow, we need to calculate the present value of $632 per month for 48 months at 1 percent per month. The loan payments are in ordinary annuity form, so the annuity present value factor is:

$$\text{Annuity PV factor} = (1 - \text{Present value factor})/r$$
$$= [1 - (1/1.01^{48})]/.01$$
$$= (1 - .6203)/.01 = 37.9740$$

With this factor, we can calculate the present value of the 48 payments of $632 each as:

$$\text{Present value} = \$632 \times 37.9740 = \$24,000$$

Therefore, $24,000 is what you can afford to borrow and repay.

Annuity Tables   Just as there are tables for ordinary present value factors, there are tables for annuity factors as well. Table 5.1 contains a few such factors; Table A.3 in Appendix A contains a larger set. To find the annuity present value factor we just calculated, look for the row corresponding to three periods and then find the column for 10 percent. The number you see at that intersection should be 2.4869 (rounded to four decimal places), as we calculated. Once again, try calculating a few of these factors yourself and compare your answers to the ones in the table to make sure you know how to do it. If you are using a financial calculator, just enter $1 as the payment and calculate the present value; the result should be the annuity present value factor.

CALCULATOR HINTS

Annuity Present Values

To find annuity present values with a financial calculator, we need to use the **PMT** key (you were probably wondering what it was for). Compared to finding the present value of a single amount, there are two important differences. First, we enter the annuity cash flow using the **PMT** key, and, second, we don't enter anything for the future value, **FV** . So, for example, the problem we have been examining is a three-year, $500 annuity. If the discount rate is 10 percent, we need to do the following (after clearing out the calculator!):

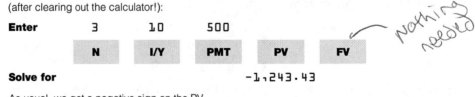

Enter	3	10	500		
	N	**I/Y**	**PMT**	**PV**	**FV**
Solve for				−1,243.43	

nothing needed

As usual, we get a negative sign on the PV.

Annuity Present Values

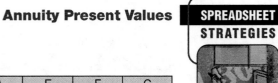

SPREADSHEET
STRATEGIES

Using a spreadsheet to work the same problem goes like this:

	A	B	C	D	E	F	G
1							
2		**Using a spreadsheet to find annuity present values**					
3							
4	What is the present value of $500 per year for 3 years if the discount rate is 10 percent?						
5	We need to solve for the unknown present value, so we use the formula PV(rate, nper, pmt, fv).						
6							
7	Payment amount per period:	$500					
8	Number of payments:	3					
9	Discount rate:	.1					
10							
11	Annuity present value:	$1,243.43					
12							
13	The formula entered in cell B11 is =PV(B9, B8, -B7, 0); notice that FV is zero and that pmt has a						
14	negative sign on it. Also notice that the discount rate is entered as a decimal, not a percentage.						
15							

Finding the Payment Suppose you wish to start up a new business that specializes in the latest of health food trends, frozen yak milk. To produce and market your product, the Yakee Doodle Dandy, you need to borrow $100,000. Because it strikes you as unlikely that this particular fad will be long-lived, you propose to pay off the loan quickly by making five equal annual payments. If the interest rate is 18 percent, what will the payments be?

In this case, we know that the present value is $100,000. The interest rate is 18 percent, and there are five years to make payments. The payments are all equal, so we need to find the relevant annuity factor and solve for the unknown cash flow:

$$\text{Annuity present value} = \$100,000 = C \times (1 - \text{Present value factor})/r$$
$$\$100,000 = C \times (1 - 1/1.18^5)/.18$$
$$= C \times (1 - .4371)/.18$$
$$= C \times 3.1272$$
$$C = \$100,000/3.1272 = \$31,978$$

Therefore, you'll make five payments of just under $32,000 each.

Annuity Payments

CALCULATOR
HINTS

Finding annuity payments is easy with a financial calculator. In our example just above, the PV is $100,000, the interest rate is 18 percent, and there are five years. We find the payment as follows:

Enter	5	18		100,000	
	N	**I/Y**	**PMT**	**PV**	**FV**
Solve for			-31,978		

Here we get a negative sign on the payment because the payment is an outflow for us.

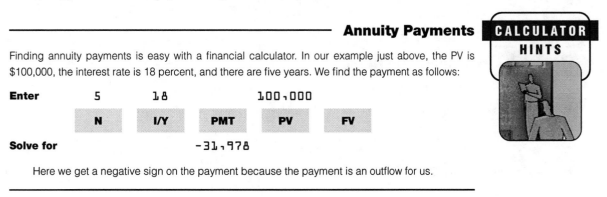

SPREADSHEET STRATEGIES

Annuity Payments

Using a spreadsheet to work the same problem goes like this:

	A	B	C	D	E	F	G
1							
2		Using a spreadsheet to find annuity payments					
3							
4	What is the annuity payment if the present value is $100,000, the interest rate is 18 percent, and						
5	there are 5 periods? We need to solve for the unknown payment in an annuity, so we use the						
6	formula PMT (rate, nper, pv, fv)						
7							
8	Annuity present value:	$100,000					
9	Number of payments:	5					
10	Discount rate:	.18					
11							
12	Annuity payment:	($31,977.78)					
13							
14	The formula entered in cell B12 is =PMT(B10, B9, -B8, 0); notice that fv is zero and that the payment						
15	has a negative sign because it is an outflow to us.						

EXAMPLE 5.6

Finding the Number of Payments

You ran a little short on your spring break vacation, so you put $1,000 on your credit card. You can only afford to make the minimum payment of $20 per month. The interest rate on the credit card is 1.5 percent per month. How long will you need to pay off the $1,000?

What we have here is an annuity of $20 per month at 1.5 percent per month for some unknown length of time. The present value is $1,000 (the amount you owe today). We need to do a little algebra (or else use a financial calculator):

$$\$1,000 = \$20 \times (1 - \text{Present value factor})/.015$$
$$(\$1,000/20) \times .015 = 1 - \text{Present value factor}$$
$$\text{Present value factor} = .25 = 1/(1 + r)^t$$
$$1.015^t = 1/.25 = 4$$

At this point, the problem boils down to asking the following question: How long does it take for your money to quadruple at 1.5 percent per month? Based on our previous chapter, the answer is about 93 months:

$$1.015^{93} = 3.99 \approx 4$$

It will take you about 93/12 = 7.75 years at this rate.

CALCULATOR HINTS

Finding the Number of Payments

To solve this one on a financial calculator, do the following:

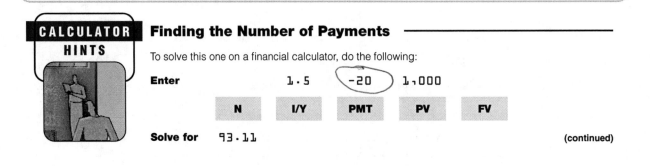

Enter		1.5	-20	1,000	
	N	**I/Y**	**PMT**	**PV**	**FV**
Solve for	93.11				

(continued)

Notice that we put a negative sign on the payment you must make, and we have solved for the number of months. You still have to divide by 12 to get our answer. Also, some financial calculators won't report a fractional value for N; they automatically (without telling you) round up to the next whole period (not to the nearest value). With a spreadsheet, use the function =NPER(rate,pmt,pv,fv); be sure to put in a zero for fv and to enter −20 as the payment.

Finding the Rate   The last question we might want to ask concerns the interest rate implicit in an annuity. For example, an insurance company offers to pay you $1,000 per year for 10 years if you pay $6,710 up front. What rate is implicit in this 10-year annuity?

In this case, we know the present value ($6,710), we know the cash flows ($1,000 per year), and we know the life of the investment (10 years). What we don't know is the discount rate:

$$\$6,710 = \$1,000 \times (1 - \text{Present value factor})/r$$
$$\$6,710/1,000 = 6.71 = \{1 - [1/(1 + r)^{10}]\}/r$$

So, the annuity factor for 10 periods is equal to 6.71, and we need to solve this equation for the unknown value of r. Unfortunately, this is mathematically impossible to do directly. The only way to do it is to use a table or trial and error to find a value for r.

If you look across the row corresponding to 10 periods in Table A.3, you will see a factor of 6.7101 for 8 percent, so we see right away that the insurance company is offering just about 8 percent. Alternatively, we could just start trying different values until we got very close to the answer. Using this trial-and-error approach can be a little tedious, but, fortunately, machines are good at that sort of thing.[1]

To illustrate how to find the answer by trial and error, suppose a relative of yours wants to borrow $3,000. She offers to repay you $1,000 every year for four years. What interest rate are you being offered?

The cash flows here have the form of a four-year, $1,000 annuity. The present value is $3,000. We need to find the discount rate, r. Our goal in doing so is primarily to give you a feel for the relationship between annuity values and discount rates.

We need to start somewhere, and 10 percent is probably as good a place as any to begin. At 10 percent, the annuity factor is:

↑ PV ↓r

Annuity present value factor = $(1 - 1/1.10^4)/.10 = 3.1699$

The present value of the cash flows at 10 percent is thus:

Present value = $\$1,000 \times 3.1699 = \$3,169.90$

You can see that we're already in the right ballpark.

Is 10 percent too high or too low? Recall that present values and discount rates move in opposite directions: Increasing the discount rate lowers the PV and vice versa. Our present value here is too high, so the discount rate is too low. If we try 12 percent:

Present value = $\$1,000 \times (1 - 1/1.12^4)/.12 = \$3,037.35$

Now we're almost there. We are still a little low on the discount rate (because the PV is a little high), so we'll try 13 percent:

Present value = $\$1,000 \times (1 - 1/1.13^4)/.13 = \$2,974.47$

---

[1]Financial calculators rely on trial and error to find the answer. That's why they sometimes appear to be "thinking" before coming up with the answer. Actually, it is possible to directly solve for r if there are fewer than five periods, but it's usually not worth the trouble.

This is less than $3,000, so we now know that the answer is between 12 percent and 13 percent, and it looks to be about 12.5 percent. For practice, work at it for a while longer and see if you find that the answer is about 12.59 percent.

Finding the Rate

Alternatively, you could use a financial calculator to do the following:

Enter	4		1,000	−3,000	
	N	**I/Y**	**PMT**	**PV**	**FV**
Solve for		12.59			

Notice that we put a negative sign on the present value (why?). With a spreadsheet, use the function =RATE(nper,pmt,pv,fv); be sure to put in a zero for fv and to enter 1,000 as the payment and −3,000 as the pv.

Future Value for Annuities

On occasion, it's also handy to know a shortcut for calculating the future value of an annuity. As you might guess, there are future value factors for annuities as well as present value factors. In general, the future value factor for an annuity is given by:

$$\text{Annuity FV factor} = (\text{Future value factor} - 1)/r$$
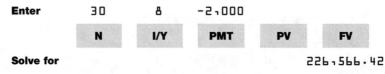
$$= [(1 + r)^t - 1]/r \times C$$

[5.2]

To see how we use annuity future value factors, suppose you plan to contribute $2,000 every year into a retirement account paying 8 percent. If you retire in 30 years, how much will you have?

The number of years here, t, is 30, and the interest rate, r, is 8 percent, so we can calculate the annuity future value factor as:

$$\text{Annuity FV factor} = (\text{Future value factor} - 1)/r$$
$$= (1.08^{30} - 1)/.08$$
$$= (10.0627 - 1)/.08$$
$$= 113.2832$$

The future value of this 30-year, $2,000 annuity is thus:

$$\text{Annuity future value} = \$2,000 \times 113.2832$$
$$= \$226,566.4$$

Future Values of Annuities

Of course, you could solve this problem using a financial calculator by doing the following:

Enter	30	8	−2,000		
	N	**I/Y**	**PMT**	**PV**	**FV**
Solve for					226,566.42

Notice that we put a negative sign on the payment (why?). With a spreadsheet, use the function =FV(rate,nper,pmt,pv); be sure to put in a zero for pv and to enter −2,000 as the payment.

A Note on Annuities Due

So far, we have only discussed ordinary annuities. These are the most important, but there is a variation that is fairly common. Remember that with an ordinary annuity, the cash flows occur at the end of each period. When you take out a loan with monthly payments, for example, the first loan payment normally occurs one month after you get the loan. However, when you lease an apartment, the first lease payment is usually due immediately. The second payment is due at the beginning of the second month, and so on. A lease is an example of an **annuity due**. An annuity due is an annuity for which the cash flows occur at the beginning of each period. Almost any type of arrangement in which we have to prepay the same amount each period is an annuity due.

annuity due

An annuity for which the cash flows occur at the beginning of the period.

There are several different ways to calculate the value of an annuity due. With a financial calculator, you simply switch it into "due" or "beginning" mode. It is very important to remember to switch it back when you are finished! Another way to calculate the present value of an annuity due can be illustrated with a time line. Suppose an annuity due has five payments of $400 each, and the relevant discount rate is 10 percent. The time line looks like this:

Notice how the cash flows here are the same as those for a *four*-year ordinary annuity, except that there is an extra $400 at Time 0. For practice, verify that the present value of a four-year $400 ordinary annuity at 10 percent is $1,267.95. If we add on the extra $400, we get $1,667.95, which is the present value of this annuity due.

There is an even easier way to calculate the present or future value of an annuity due. If we assume that cash flows occur at the end of each period when they really occur at the beginning, then we discount each one by one period too many. We could fix this by simply multiplying our answer by $(1 + r)$, where r is the discount rate. In fact, the relationship between the value of an annuity due and an ordinary annuity with the same number of payments is just:

Time value applications abound on the Web. See, for example, **www.collegeboard. com, www. 1stmortgagedirectory. com,** and **personal.fidelity.com**.

$$\text{Annuity due value} = \text{Ordinary annuity value} \times (1 + r) \qquad [5.3]$$

This works for both present and future values, so calculating the value of an annuity due involves two steps: (1) calculate the present or future value as though it were an ordinary annuity and (2) multiply your answer by $(1 + r)$.

Perpetuities

We've seen that a series of level cash flows can be valued by treating those cash flows as an annuity. An important special case of an annuity arises when the level stream of cash flows continues forever. Such an asset is called a **perpetuity** since the cash flows are perpetual. Perpetuities are also called **consols**, particularly in Canada and the United Kingdom. See Example 5.7 for an important example of a perpetuity.

Since a perpetuity has an infinite number of cash flows, we obviously can't compute its value by discounting each one. Fortunately, valuing a perpetuity turns out to be the easiest possible case. The present value of a perpetuity is simply:

perpetuity

An annuity in which the cash flows continue forever.

consol

A type of perpetuity.

$$\text{PV for a perpetuity} = C/r \qquad [5.4]$$

For example, an investment offers a perpetual cash flow of $500 every year. The return you require on such an investment is 8 percent. What is the value of this investment? The value

TABLE 5.2

Summary of annuity and perpetuity calculations

I. **Symbols**
   PV = Present value, what future cash flows are worth today
   FV_t = Future value, what cash flows are worth in the future at time t
   r = Interest rate, rate of return, or discount rate per period—typically, but not always, one year
   t = Number of periods—typically, but not always, the number of years
   C = Cash amount

II. **Future value of C invested per period for t periods at r percent per period**
   $FV_t = C \times [(1 + r)^t - 1]/r$
   A series of identical cash flows is called an annuity, and the term $[(1 + r)^t - 1]/r$ is called the *annuity future value factor*.

III. **Present value of C per period for t periods at r percent per period**
   $PV = C \times \{1 - [1/(1 + r)^t]\}/r$
   The term $\{1 - [1/(1 + r)^t]\}/r$ is called the *annuity present value factor*.

IV. **Present value of a perpetuity of C per period**
   $PV = C/r$
   A perpetuity has the same cash flow every year forever.

of this perpetuity is:

Perpetuity PV = C/r = $500/.08 = $6,250

This concludes our discussion of valuing investments with multiple cash flows. For future reference, Table 5.2 contains a summary of the annuity and perpetuity basic calculations we described. By now, you probably think that you'll just use online calculators to handle annuity problems. Before you do, see our nearby *Work the Web* box.

WORK THE WEB

As we discussed in our previous chapter, many Web sites have financial calculators. One of these sites is MoneyChimp, which is located at www.moneychimp.com. Suppose you retire with $1,000,000 and want to withdraw an equal amount each year for the next 30 years. If you can earn a 9 percent return, how much can you withdraw each year? Here is what MoneyChimp says:

Inputs		
Starting Principal:	$	1,000,000.00
Growth Rate:		9 %
Years to Pay Out:		30
	Calculate	
Results		
Annual Payout Amount:	$	89,299.40

According to the MoneyChimp calculator, the answer is $89,299.40. How important is it to understand what you are doing? Calculate this one for yourself, and you should get $97,336.35. Which one is right? You are, of course! What's going on is that MoneyChimp assumes (but tells you on a different page) that the annuity is in the form of an annuity due, not an ordinary annuity. Recall that with an annuity due the payments occur at the beginning of the period rather than at the end of the period. The moral of the story is clear: *Caveat calculator.*

Preferred Stock   EXAMPLE 5.7

Preferred stock (or preference stock) is an important example of a perpetuity. When a corporation sells preferred stock, the buyer is promised a fixed cash dividend every period (usually every quarter) forever. This dividend must be paid before any dividend can be paid to regular stockholders, hence the term *preferred.*

Suppose the Fellini Co. wants to sell preferred stock at $100 per share. A very similar issue of preferred stock already outstanding has a price of $40 per share and offers a dividend of $1 every quarter. What dividend will Fellini have to offer if the preferred stock is going to sell?

The issue that is already out has a present value of $40 and a cash flow of $1 every quarter forever. Since this is a perpetuity:

Present value = $40 = $1 × (1/r)
$r = 2.5\%$

To be competitive, the new Fellini issue will also have to offer 2.5 percent *per quarter;* so, if the present value is to be $100, the dividend must be such that:

Present value = $100 = C × (1/.025)
C = $2.5 (per quarter)

CONCEPT QUESTIONS

5.2a In general, what is the present value of an annuity of *C* dollars per period at a discount rate of *r* per period? The future value?

5.2b In general, what is the present value of a perpetuity?

COMPARING RATES: THE EFFECT OF COMPOUNDING PERIODS   5.3

The last issue we need to discuss has to do with the way interest rates are quoted. This subject causes a fair amount of confusion because rates are quoted in many different ways. Sometimes the way a rate is quoted is the result of tradition, and sometimes it's the result of legislation. Unfortunately, at times, rates are quoted in deliberately deceptive ways to mislead borrowers and investors. We will discuss these topics in this section.

Effective Annual Rates and Compounding

If a rate is quoted as 10 percent compounded semiannually, then what this means is that the investment actually pays 5 percent every six months. A natural question then arises: Is 5 percent every six months the same thing as 10 percent per year? It's easy to see that it is not. If you invest $1 at 10 percent per year, you will have $1.10 at the end of the year. If you invest at 5 percent every six months, then you'll have the future value of $1 at 5 percent for two periods, or:

$$\$1 \times 1.05^2 = \$1.1025$$

This is $.0025 more. The reason is very simple. What has occurred is that your account was credited with $1 × .05 = 5 cents in interest after six months. In the following six months, you earned 5 percent on that nickel, for an extra 5 × .05 = .25 cent.

As our example illustrates, 10 percent compounded semiannually is actually equivalent to 10.25 percent per year. Put another way, we would be indifferent between 10 percent compounded semiannually and 10.25 percent compounded annually. Anytime we have compounding during the year, we need to be concerned about what the rate really is.

In our example, the 10 percent is called a **stated**, or **quoted**, **interest rate**. Other names are used as well. The 10.25 percent, which is actually the rate that you will earn, is called the **effective annual rate (EAR)**. To compare different investments or interest rates, we will always need to convert to effective rates. Some general procedures for doing this are discussed next.

stated interest rate

The interest rate expressed in terms of the interest payment made each period. Also, quoted interest rate.

effective annual rate (EAR)

The interest rate expressed as if it were compounded once per year.

Calculating and Comparing Effective Annual Rates

To see why it is important to work only with effective rates, suppose you've shopped around and come up with the following three rates:

Bank A: 15 percent, compounded daily   .15/365

Bank B: 15.5 percent, compounded quarterly   .155/4

Bank C: 16 percent, compounded annually   .16

Which of these is the best if you are thinking of opening a savings account? Which of these is best if they represent loan rates?

To begin, Bank C is offering 16 percent per year. Since there is no compounding during the year, this is the effective rate. Bank B is actually paying $.155/4 = .03875$, or 3.875 percent, per quarter. At this rate, an investment of $1 for four quarters would grow to:

$$\$1 \times 1.03875^4 = \$1.1642$$

The EAR, therefore, is 16.42 percent. For a saver, this is much better than the 16 percent rate Bank C is offering; for a borrower, it's worse.

Bank A is compounding every day. This may seem a little extreme, but it is very common to calculate interest daily. In this case, the daily interest rate is actually:

$$.15/365 = .000411$$

This is .0411 percent per day. At this rate, an investment of $1 for 365 periods would grow to:

$$\$1 \times 1.000411^{365} = \$1.1618$$

The EAR is 16.18 percent. This is not as good as Bank B's 16.42 percent for a saver, and not as good as Bank C's 16 percent for a borrower.

This example illustrates two things. First, the highest quoted rate is not necessarily the best. Second, compounding during the year can lead to a significant difference between the quoted rate and the effective rate. Remember that the effective rate is what you get or what you pay.

If you look at our examples, you see that we computed the EARs in three steps. We first divided the quoted rate by the number of times that the interest is compounded. We then added 1 to the result and raised it to the power of the number of times the interest is compounded. Finally, we subtracted the 1. If we let m be the number of times the interest is compounded during the year, these steps can be summarized simply as:

$$EAR = (1 + \text{Quoted rate}/m)^m - 1 \qquad \text{[5.5]}$$

For example, suppose you were offered 12 percent compounded monthly. In this case, the interest is compounded 12 times a year; so m is 12. You can calculate the effective rate as:

$$EAR = (1 + \text{Quoted rate}/m)^m - 1$$
$$= (1 + .12/12)^{12} - 1$$
$$= 1.01^{12} - 1$$
$$= 1.126825 - 1$$
$$= 12.6825\%$$

What's the EAR? EXAMPLE 5.8

A bank is offering 12 percent compounded quarterly. If you put $100 in an account, how much will you have at the end of one year? What's the EAR? How much will you have at the end of two years?

The bank is effectively offering 12%/4 = 3% every quarter. If you invest $100 for four periods at 3 percent per period, the future value is:

Future value = $100 × 1.03⁴
= $100 × 1.1255
= $112.55

$$\left[\left(1 + \frac{.12}{4}\right)^4 - 1\right] \times 100$$
$$= 12.55\%$$

The EAR is 12.55 percent: $100 × (1 + .1255) = $112.55.

We can determine what you would have at the end of two years in two different ways. One way is to recognize that two years is the same as eight quarters. At 3 percent per quarter, after eight quarters, you would have:

$100 × 1.03⁸ = $100 × 1.2668 = $126.68   *8 quarters*

Alternatively, we could determine the value after two years by using an EAR of 12.55 percent; so after two years you would have:

$100 × 1.1255² = $100 × 1.2688 = $126.68   *2 years*

Thus, the two calculations produce the same answer. This illustrates an important point. Anytime we do a present or future value calculation, the rate we use must be an actual or effective rate. In this case, the actual rate is 3 percent per quarter. The effective annual rate is 12.55 percent. It doesn't matter which one we use once we know the EAR.

Quoting a Rate EXAMPLE 5.9

Now that you know how to convert a quoted rate to an EAR, consider going the other way. As a lender, you know you want to actually earn 18 percent on a particular loan. You want to quote a rate that features monthly compounding. What rate do you quote?

In this case, we know that the EAR is 18 percent, and we know that this is the result of monthly compounding. Let q stand for the quoted rate. We thus have:

$$EAR = (1 + \text{Quoted rate}/m)^m - 1$$
$$.18 = (1 + q/12)^{12} - 1$$
$$1.18 = (1 + q/12)^{12}$$

(continued)

We need to solve this equation for the quoted rate. This calculation is the same as the ones we did to find an unknown interest rate in Chapter 4:

$$1.18^{(1/12)} = 1 + q/12$$
$$1.18^{.08333} = 1 + q/12$$
$$1.0139 = 1 + q/12$$
$$q = .0139 \times 12$$
$$= 16.68\%$$

Therefore, the rate you would quote is 16.68 percent, compounded monthly.

EARs and APRs

annual percentage rate (APR)

The interest rate charged per period multiplied by the number of periods per year.

Sometimes it's not altogether clear whether a rate is an effective annual rate or not. A case in point concerns what is called the **annual percentage rate (APR)** on a loan. Truth-in-lending laws in the United States require that lenders disclose an APR on virtually all consumer loans. This rate must be displayed on a loan document in a prominent and unambiguous way.

Given that an APR must be calculated and displayed, an obvious question arises: Is an APR an effective annual rate? Put another way: If a bank quotes a car loan at 12 percent APR, is the consumer actually paying 12 percent interest? Surprisingly, the answer is no. There is some confusion over this point, which we discuss next.

The confusion over APRs arises because lenders are required by law to compute the APR in a particular way. By law, the APR is simply equal to the interest rate per period multiplied by the number of periods in a year. For example, if a bank is charging 1.2 percent per month on car loans, then the APR that must be reported is $1.2\% \times 12 = 14.4\%$. So, an APR is in fact a quoted, or stated, rate in the sense we've been discussing. For example, an APR of 12 percent on a loan calling for monthly payments is really 1 percent per month. The EAR on such a loan is thus:

$$EAR = (1 + APR/12)^{12} - 1$$
$$= 1.01^{12} - 1 = 12.6825\%$$

EXAMPLE 5.10   **What Rate Are You Paying?**

A typical credit card agreement quotes an interest rate of 18 percent APR. Monthly payments are required. What is the actual interest rate you pay on such a credit card?

Based on our discussion, an APR of 18 percent with monthly payments is really .18/12 = .015, or 1.5 percent, per month. The EAR is thus:

$$EAR = (1 + .18/12)^{12} - 1$$
$$= 1.015^{12} - 1$$
$$= 1.1956 - 1$$
$$= 19.56\%$$

This is the rate you actually pay.

The difference between an APR and an EAR probably won't be all that great (as long as the rates are relatively low), but it is somewhat ironic that truth-in-lending laws sometimes require lenders to be *un*truthful about the actual rate on a loan.

There can be a huge difference between the APR and EAR when interest rates are large. For example, consider "payday loans." Payday loans are short-term loans made to consumers, often for less than two weeks, and are offered by companies such as AmeriCash Advance and National Payday. The loans work like this: You write a check today that is postdated (i.e., the date on the check is in the future) and give it to the company. They give you some cash. When the check date arrives, you either go to the store and pay the cash amount of the check, or the company cashes it (or else automatically renews the loan).

For example, AmeriCash Advance allows you to write a check for $125 dated 15 days in the future, for which they give you $100 today. So what is the APR and EAR of this arrangement? First we need to find the interest rate, which we can find by the FV equation as:

$$FV = PV \times (1 + r)^1$$
$$\$125 = \$100 \times (1 + r)^1$$
$$1.25 = (1 + r)$$
$$r = .25 \text{ or } 25\%$$

That doesn't seem too bad until you remember this is the interest rate for *15 days!* The APR of the loan is:

$$APR = .25 \times 365/15$$
$$APR = 6.08333 \text{ or } 608.33\%$$

And the EAR for this loan is:

$$EAR = (1 + \text{Quoted rate}/m)^m - 1$$
$$EAR = (1 + .25)^{365/15} - 1$$
$$EAR = 227.1096 \text{ or } 22,710.96\%$$

Now that's an interest rate! Just to see what a difference a day (or three) makes, let's look at National Payday's terms. This company will allow you to write a postdated check for the same amount, but will give you 18 days to repay. Check for yourself that the APR of this arrangement is 506.94 percent and the EAR is 9,128.26 percent. Still not a loan we would like to take out!

EARs, APRs, Financial Calculators, and Spreadsheets

A financial calculator will convert a quoted rate (or an APR) to an EAR and back. Unfortunately, the specific procedures are too different from calculator to calculator for us to illustrate in general terms; you'll have to consult Appendix D or your calculator's operating manual. Typically, however, what we have called EAR is labeled "EFF" (for *effective*) on a calculator. More troublesome is the fact that what we have called a quoted rate (or an APR) is labeled "NOM" (for *nominal*). Unfortunately, the term *nominal rate* has come to have a different meaning that we will see in our next chapter. So, just remember that *nominal* in this context means quoted or APR.

With a spreadsheet, we can easily do these conversions. To convert a quoted rate (or an APR) to an effective rate in Excel, for example, use the formula EFFECT(nominal_rate,npery), where nominal_rate is the quoted rate or APR and npery is the number of compounding periods per year. Similarly, to convert an EAR to a quoted rate, use NOMINAL(effect_rate,npery), where effect_rate is the EAR.

5.4 | LOAN TYPES AND LOAN AMORTIZATION

Whenever a lender extends a loan, some provision will be made for repayment of the principal (the original loan amount). A loan might be repaid in equal installments, for example, or it might be repaid in a single lump sum. Because the way that the principal and interest are paid is up to the parties involved, there are actually an unlimited number of possibilities.

In this section, we describe a few forms of repayment that come up quite often; more complicated forms can usually be built up from these. The three basic types of loans are pure discount loans, interest-only loans, and amortized loans. Working with these loans is a very straightforward application of the present value principles that we have already developed.

Pure Discount Loans

The pure discount loan is the simplest form of loan. With such a loan, the borrower receives money today and repays a single lump sum at some time in the future. A one-year, 10 percent pure discount loan, for example, would require the borrower to repay $1.1 in one year for every dollar borrowed today.

Because a pure discount loan is so simple, we already know how to value one. Suppose a borrower was able to repay $25,000 in five years. If we, acting as the lender, wanted a 12 percent interest rate on the loan, how much would we be willing to lend? Put another way, what value would we assign today to that $25,000 to be repaid in five years? Based on our work in Chapter 4, we know that the answer is just the present value of $25,000 at 12 percent for five years:

$$\text{Present value} = \$25,000/1.12^5$$
$$= \$25,000/1.7623$$
$$= \$14,186$$

Pure discount loans are very common when the loan term is short, say, a year or less. In recent years, they have become increasingly common for much longer periods.

EXAMPLE 5.11   **Treasury Bills**

When the U.S. government borrows money on a short-term basis (a year or less), it does so by selling what are called *Treasury bills,* or *T-bills* for short. A T-bill is a promise by the government to repay a fixed amount at some time in the future, for example, 3 months or 12 months.

Treasury bills are pure discount loans. If a T-bill promises to repay $10,000 in 12 months, and the market interest rate is 7 percent, how much will the bill sell for in the market?

Since the going rate is 7 percent, the T-bill will sell for the present value of $10,000 to be paid in one year at 7 percent, or:

Present value = $10,000/1.07 = $9,345.79

Interest-Only Loans

A second type of loan has a repayment plan that calls for the borrower to pay interest each period and to repay the entire principal (the original loan amount) at some point in the future. Such loans are called *interest-only loans*. Notice that if there is just one period, a pure discount loan and an interest-only loan are the same thing.

For example, with a three-year, 10 percent, interest-only loan of $1,000, the borrower would pay $1,000 × .10 = $100 in interest at the end of the first and second years. At the end of the third year, the borrower would return the $1,000 along with another $100 in interest for that year. Similarly, a 50-year interest-only loan would call for the borrower to pay interest every year for the next 50 years and then repay the principal. In the extreme, the borrower pays the interest every period forever and never repays any principal. As we discussed earlier in the chapter, the result is a perpetuity.

Most corporate bonds have the general form of an interest-only loan. Because we will be considering bonds in some detail in the next chapter, we will defer a further discussion of them for now.

Amortized Loans

With a pure discount or interest-only loan, the principal is repaid all at once. An alternative is an *amortized loan,* with which the lender may require the borrower to repay parts of the loan amount over time. The process of paying off a loan by making regular principal reductions is called *amortizing* the loan.

A simple way of amortizing a loan is to have the borrower pay the interest each period plus some fixed amount. This approach is common with medium-term business loans. For example, suppose a business takes out a $5,000, five-year loan at 9 percent. The loan agreement calls for the borrower to pay the interest on the loan balance each year and to reduce the loan balance each year by $1,000. Since the loan amount declines by $1,000 each year, it is fully paid in five years.

In the case we are considering, notice that the total payment will decline each year. The reason is that the loan balance goes down, resulting in a lower interest charge each year, while the $1,000 principal reduction is constant. For example, the interest in the first year will be $5,000 × .09 = $450. The total payment will be $1,000 + 450 = $1,450. In the second year, the loan balance is $4,000, so the interest is $4,000 × .09 = $360, and the total payment is $1,360. We can calculate the total payment in each of the remaining years by preparing a simple *amortization schedule* as follows:

Year	Beginning Balance	Total Payment	Interest Paid	Principal Paid	Ending Balance
1	$5,000	$1,450	$ 450	$1,000	$4,000
2	4,000	1,360	360	1,000	3,000
3	3,000	1,270	270	1,000	2,000
4	2,000	1,180	180	1,000	1,000
5	1,000	1,090	90	1,000	0
Totals		$6,350	$1,350	$5,000	

Notice that, in each year, the interest paid is just given by the beginning balance multiplied by the interest rate. Also notice that the beginning balance is given by the ending balance from the previous year.

Probably the most common way of amortizing a loan is to have the borrower make a single, fixed payment every period. Almost all consumer loans (such as car loans) and mortgages work this way. For example, suppose our five-year, 9 percent, $5,000 loan was amortized this way. How would the amortization schedule look?

We first need to determine the payment. From our discussion earlier in the chapter, we know that this loan's cash flows are in the form of an ordinary annuity. In this case, we can solve for the payment as follows:

$$\$5,000 = C \times (1 - 1/1.09^5)/.09$$
$$= C \times (1 - .6499)/.09$$

This gives us:

$$C = \$5,000/3.8897$$
$$= \$1,285.46$$

The borrower will therefore make five equal payments of $1,285.46. Will this pay off the loan? We will check by filling in an amortization schedule.

In our previous example, we knew the principal reduction each year. We then calculated the interest owed to get the total payment. In this example, we know the total payment. We will thus calculate the interest and then subtract it from the total payment to get the principal portion in each payment.

In the first year, the interest is $450, as we calculated before. Since the total payment is $1,285.46, the principal paid in the first year must be:

$$\text{Principal paid} = \$1,285.46 - 450 = \$835.46$$

The ending loan balance is thus:

$$\text{Ending balance} = \$5,000 - 835.46 = \$4,164.54$$

The interest in the second year is $4,164.54 \times .09 = \$374.81$, and the loan balance declines by $1,285.46 - 374.81 = \$910.65$. We can summarize all of the relevant calculations in the following schedule:

Year	Beginning Balance	Total Payment	Interest Paid	Principal Paid	Ending Balance
1	$5,000.00	$1,285.46	$ 450.00	$ 835.46	$4,164.54
2	4,164.54	1,285.46	374.81	910.65	3,253.88
3	3,253.88	1,285.46	292.85	992.61	2,261.27
4	2,261.27	1,285.46	203.51	1,081.95	1,179.32
5	1,179.32	1,285.46	106.14	1,179.32	.00
Totals		$6,427.30	$1,427.31	$5,000.00	

Since the loan balance declines to zero, the five equal payments do pay off the loan. Notice that the interest paid declines each period. This isn't surprising since the loan balance is going down. Given that the total payment is fixed, the principal paid must be rising each period.

If you compare the two loan amortizations in this section, you will see that the total interest is greater for the equal total payment case, $1,427.31 versus $1,350. The reason for this is that the loan is repaid more slowly early on, so the interest is somewhat higher. This doesn't mean that one loan is better than the other; it simply means that one is effectively paid off faster than the other. For example, the principal reduction in the first year is $835.46 in the equal total payment case compared to $1,000 in the first case. Many Web sites offer loan amortization schedules. See our nearby *Work the Web* box for an example.

Loan Amortization Using a Spreadsheet

SPREADSHEET STRATEGIES

Loan amortization is a very common spreadsheet application. To illustrate, we will set up the problem that we have just examined, a five-year, $5,000, 9 percent loan with constant payments. Our spreadsheet looks like this:

	A	B	C	D	E	F	G	H
1								
2				Using a spreadsheet to amortize a loan				
3								
4			Loan amount:	$5,000				
5			Interest rate:	.09				
6			Loan term:	5				
7			Loan payment:	**$1,285.46**				
8				Note: payment is calculated using PMT(rate,nper,-pv,fv).				
9			Amortization table:					
10								
11		Year	Beginning	Total	Interest	Principal	Ending	
12			Balance	Payment	Paid	Paid	Balance	
13		1	$5,000.00	$1,285.46	$450.00	$835.46	$4,164.54	
14		2	4,164.54	1,285.46	374.81	910.65	3,253.88	
15		3	3,253.88	1,285.46	292.85	992.61	2,261.27	
16		4	2,261.27	1,285.46	203.51	1,081.95	1,179.32	
17		5	1,179.32	1,285.46	106.14	1,179.32	.00	
18		Totals		$6,427.31	$1,427.31	$5,000.00		
19								
20		Formulas in the amortization table:						
21								
22		Year	Beginning	Total	Interest	Principal	Ending	
23			Balance	Payment	Paid	Paid	Balance	
24		1	=+D4	=$D$7	=+$D$5*C13	=+D13-E13	=+C13-F13	
25		2	=+G13	=$D$7	=+$D$5*C14	=+D14-E14	=+C14-F14	
26		3	=+G14	=$D$7	=+$D$5*C15	=+D15-E15	=+C15-F15	
27		4	=+G15	=$D$7	=+$D$5*C16	=+D16-E16	=+C16-F16	
28		5	=+G16	=$D$7	=+$D$5*C17	=+D17-E17	=+C17-F17	
29								
30		Note: totals in the amortization table are calculated using the SUM formula.						
31								

Preparing an amortization table is one of the more tedious time value of money applications. Using a spreadsheet makes it relatively easy, but there are also Web sites available that will prepare an amortization table very quickly and simply. One such site is LendingTree. Their Web site at www.lendingtree.com has a mortgage calculator for home loans, but the same calculations apply to most other types of loans such as car loans and student loans. Suppose you graduate with a student loan of $30,000 and will repay the loan over the next 15 years at 5.99 percent. What are your monthly payments? Using the calculator we get:

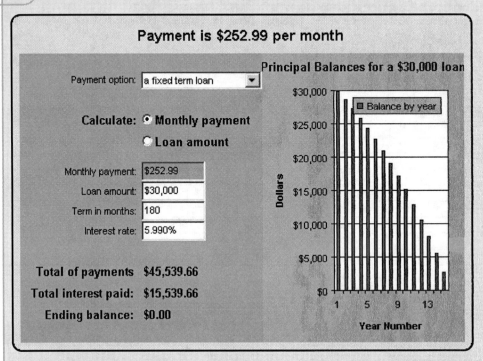

Try this example yourself and hit the "View Report" button. You will find that your first payment will consist of $103.24 in principal and $149.75 in interest. Over the life of the loan you will pay a total of $15,539.66 in interest.

We close out this discussion by noting that one type of loan may be particularly important to you. Student loans are an important source of financing for many college students, helping to cover the cost of tuition, books, new cars, condominiums, and many other things. Sometimes students do not seem to fully realize that such loans have a serious drawback: They must be repaid. See our nearby *Reality Bytes* box for a discussion.

CONCEPT QUESTIONS

5.4a   What is a pure discount loan?

5.4b   What does it mean to amortize a loan?

An Unwelcome Christmas Present

If you are reading this, we can assume that you are a college student. While you will receive an education in college, and studies show that college graduates earn a higher salary on average than nongraduates, you might receive an unwelcome Christmas present if you graduate in May: student loan payments. About one-half of all college students graduate with student loans, and over 90 percent of the loans are Stafford loans. Stafford loans are available through lenders such as Sallie Mae, online lenders, or, in some cases, your college. Stafford loans must be paid off in 10 years, but there is a six-month grace period from the time you graduate until the first payment must be made. The good news is that the current interest rate for money borrowed since 1998 is 5.99 percent, the lowest in the 36-year history of the Stafford loan program.

If you have student loans, you went through an introductory program. Just in case you forgot, here are several of the repayment options. First, you can make equal monthly payments like most other loans. A second option is to pay only the interest on the loan for up to four years, and then begin making principal and interest payments. This means your payments at the end of the loan are higher than the equal payment option. A third option is to make payments based on a percentage of your salary. A fourth option is a graduated payment option that increases your monthly payments on a predetermined schedule. Finally, you can consolidate your loans one time. If the loan balance is high enough, you may be able to extend your payment for up to 30 years.

So how do student loans work in practice? A recent graduate from the University of Maryland with a master's degree in creative writing graduated with $40,000 in student loans. Her loan payments were $442 a month, a payment that was difficult to make on her salary as a fundraiser. She considered the percentage of salary option, which would have lowered her monthly payments to about $200 per month. However, she realized that this was just putting off the inevitable, so she took a second job to make up the difference.

A recent master's graduate from law school took a different route. His student loans totaled $109,000 and required monthly payments of $1,200 per month for 10 years. The option chosen by this lawyer was to consolidate his loans and extend his payments to 30 years. This reduced his monthly payments to about $640 per month.

A Chicago couple is using a third solution. Both the husband and wife are doctors. The wife is out of her residency and employed full time, while the husband is finishing his last year of residency. What is most unusual about this couple is the amount of student loan debt. The wife's student loan balance is $234,000, the husband's student loan balance is $310,000, and the couple has a $156,000 mortgage! The wife's student loan repayments have already started and amount to $1,750 per month. So how is the couple handling this? They are paying a total of $2,250 per month towards the wife's student loans. This will reduce the repayment period from 22 years to 13 years. The couple is also paying an additional $100 per month on their $1,500 mortgage payment. Fortunately, when the husband's residency ends, he expects his salary to triple. The couple will need it. His loan payments will be $2,349 per month. And you thought your student loan was high! Maybe MD stands for "mucho debt"!

SUMMARY AND CONCLUSIONS

This chapter rounds out your understanding of fundamental concepts related to the time value of money and discounted cash flow valuation. Several important topics were covered, including:

1. There are two ways of calculating present and future values when there are multiple cash flows. Both approaches are straightforward extensions of our earlier analysis of single cash flows.

2. A series of constant cash flows that arrive or are paid at the end of each period is called an ordinary annuity, and we described some useful shortcuts for determining the present and future values of annuities.

3. Interest rates can be quoted in a variety of ways. For financial decisions, it is important that any rates being compared be first converted to effective rates. The

relationship between a quoted rate, such as an annual percentage rate, or APR, and an effective annual rate, or EAR, is given by:

$$EAR = (1 + \text{Quoted rate}/m)^m - 1$$

where m is the number of times during the year the money is compounded, or, equivalently, the number of payments during the year.

4. Many loans are annuities. The process of paying off a loan gradually is called amortizing the loan, and we discussed how amortization schedules are prepared and interpreted.

CHAPTER REVIEW AND SELF-TEST PROBLEMS

5.1   Present Values with Multiple Cash Flows.   A first-round draft choice quarterback has been signed to a three-year, $10 million contract. The details provide for an immediate cash bonus of $1 million. The player is to receive $2 million in salary at the end of the first year, $3 million the next, and $4 million at the end of the last year. Assuming a 10 percent discount rate, is this package worth $10 million? How much is it worth?

5.2   Future Value with Multiple Cash Flows.   You plan to make a series of deposits in an interest-bearing account. You will deposit $1,000 today, $2,000 in two years, and $8,000 in five years. If you withdraw $3,000 in three years and $5,000 in seven years, how much will you have after eight years if the interest rate is 9 percent? What is the present value of these cash flows?

5.3   Annuity Present Value.   You are looking into an investment that will pay you $12,000 per year for the next 10 years. If you require a 15 percent return, what is the most you would pay for this investment?

5.4   APR versus EAR.   The going rate on student loans is quoted as 9 percent APR. The terms of the loan call for monthly payments. What is the effective annual rate, or EAR, on such a student loan?

5.5   It's the Principal That Matters.   Suppose you borrow $10,000. You are going to repay the loan by making equal annual payments for five years. The interest rate on the loan is 14 percent per year. Prepare an amortization schedule for the loan. How much interest will you pay over the life of the loan?

5.6   Just a Little Bit Each Month.   You've recently finished your MBA at the Darnit School. Naturally, you must purchase a new BMW immediately. The car costs about $21,000. The bank quotes an interest rate of 15 percent APR for a 72-month loan with a 10 percent down payment. What will your monthly payment be? What is the effective interest rate on the loan?

▨ Answers to Chapter Review and Self-Test Problems

5.1   Obviously, the package is not worth $10 million because the payments are spread out over three years. The bonus is paid today, so it's worth $1 million. The present values for the three subsequent salary payments are:

$$\$2/1.1 + 3/1.1^2 + 4/1.1^3 \quad = \$2/1.1 + 3/1.21 + 4/1.331$$
$$= \$7.3028$$

The package is worth a total of $8.3028 million.

5.2 We will calculate the future value for each of the cash flows separately and then add the results up. Notice that we treat the withdrawals as negative cash flows:

$$
\begin{array}{rll}
\$1{,}000 \times 1.09^8 = & \$1{,}000 \times 1.9926 = \$ & 1{,}992.60 \\
\$2{,}000 \times 1.09^6 = & \$2{,}000 \times 1.6771 = & 3{,}354.20 \\
-\$3{,}000 \times 1.09^5 = & -\$3{,}000 \times 1.5386 = & -4{,}615.87 \\
\$8{,}000 \times 1.09^3 = & \$8{,}000 \times 1.2950 = & 10{,}360.23 \\
-\$5{,}000 \times 1.09^1 = & -\$5{,}000 \times 1.0900 = & \underline{-5{,}450.00} \\
& \text{Total future value} = \$ & 5{,}641.12
\end{array}
$$

This value includes a small rounding error.

To calculate the present value, we could discount each cash flow back to the present or we could discount back a single year at a time. However, since we already know that the future value in eight years is $5,641.12, the easy way to get the PV is just to discount this amount back eight years:

Present value = $5,641.12/1.09^8
= $5,641.12/1.9926
= $2,831.03

We again ignore a small rounding error. For practice, you can verify that this is what you get if you discount each cash flow back separately.

5.3 The most you would be willing to pay is the present value of $12,000 per year for 10 years at a 15 percent discount rate. The cash flows here are in ordinary annuity form, so the relevant present value factor is:

Annuity present value factor = [1 − (1/1.15^10)]/.15
= (1 − .2472)/.15
= 5.0188

The present value of the 10 cash flows is thus:

Present value = $12,000 × 5.0188
= $60,225

This is the most you would pay.

5.4 A rate of 9 percent with monthly payments is actually 9%/12 = .75% per month. The EAR is thus:

EAR = (1 + .09/12)^{12} − 1 = 9.38%

5.5 We first need to calculate the annual payment. With a present value of $10,000, an interest rate of 14 percent, and a term of five years, the payment can be determined from:

$10,000 = Payment × (1 − 1/1.14^5)/.14
= Payment × 3.4331

Therefore, the payment is $10,000/3.4331 = $2,912.84 (actually, it's $2,912.8355; this will create some small rounding errors in the schedule below). We can now prepare the amortization schedule as follows:

Year	Beginning Balance	Total Payment	Interest Paid	Principal Paid	Ending Balance
1	$10,000.00	$ 2,912.84	$1,400.00	$ 1,512.84	$8,487.16
2	8,487.16	2,912.84	1,188.20	1,724.63	6,762.53
3	6,762.53	2,912.84	946.75	1,966.08	4,796.45
4	4,796.45	2,912.84	671.50	2,241.33	2,555.12
5	2,555.12	2,912.84	357.72	2,555.12	.00
Totals		$14,564.17	$4,564.17	$10,000.00	

5.6 The cash flows on the car loan are in annuity form, so we only need to find the payment. The interest rate is $15\%/12 = 1.25\%$ per month, and there are 72 months. The first thing we need is the annuity factor for 72 periods at 1.25 percent per period:

$$\begin{aligned}
\text{Annuity present value factor} &= (1 - \text{Present value factor})/r \\
&= [1 - (1/1.0125^{72})]/.0125 \\
&= [1 - (1/2.4459)]/.0125 \\
&= (1 - .4088)/.0125 \\
&= 47.2925
\end{aligned}$$

The present value is the amount we finance. With a 10 percent down payment, we will be borrowing 90 percent of $21,000, or $18,900.

So, to find the payment, we need to solve for C in the following:

$$\begin{aligned}
\$18,900 &= C \times \text{Annuity present value factor} \\
&= C \times 47.2925
\end{aligned}$$

Rearranging things a bit, we have:

$$\begin{aligned}
C &= \$18,900 \times (1/47.2925) \\
&= \$18,900 \times .02115 \\
&= \$399.64
\end{aligned}$$

Your payment is just under $400 per month.

The actual interest rate on this loan is 1.25 percent per month. Based on our work in the chapter, we can calculate the effective annual rate as:

$$EAR = 1.0125^{12} - 1 = 16.08\%$$

The effective rate is about one point higher than the quoted rate.

CRITICAL THINKING AND CONCEPTS REVIEW

5.1 **Annuity Period.** As you increase the length of time involved, what happens to the present value of an annuity? What happens to the future value?

5.2 **Interest Rates.** What happens to the future value of an annuity if you increase the rate r? What happens to the present value?

5.3 **Annuity Present Values.** Tri-State Megabucks Lottery advertises a $10 million dollar grand prize. The winner receives $500,000 today and 19 annual payments of $500,000. A lump sum option of $5 million payable immediately is also available. Is this deceptive advertising?

5.4   **Annuity Present Values.**   Suppose you won the Tri-State Megabucks Lottery in the previous question. What factors should you take into account in deciding whether you should take the annuity option or the lump sum option?

5.5   **Present Value.**   If you were an athlete negotiating a contract, would you want a big signing bonus payable immediately and smaller payments in the future, or vice versa? How about looking at it from the team's perspective?

5.6   **Present Value.**   Suppose two athletes sign 10-year contracts for $80 million. In one case, we're told that the $80 million will be paid in 10 equal installments. In the other case, we're told that the $80 million will be paid in 10 installments, but the installments will increase by 5 percent per year. Who got the better deal?

5.7   **APR and EAR.**   Should lending laws be changed to require lenders to report EARs instead of APRs? Why or why not?

5.8   **Time Value.**   On subsidized Stafford loans, a common source of financial aid for college students, interest does not begin to accrue until repayment begins. Who receives a bigger subsidy, a freshman or a senior? Explain.

5.9   **Time Value.**   In words, how would you go about valuing the subsidy on a subsidized Stafford loan?

5.10   **Time Value.**   Eligibility for a subsidized Stafford loan is based on current financial need. However, both subsidized and unsubsidized Stafford loans are repaid out of future income. Given this, do you see a possible objection to having two types?

QUESTIONS AND PROBLEMS

1. **Present Value and Multiple Cash Flows.**   Ancelet Co. has identified an investment project with the following cash flows. If the discount rate is 10 percent, what is the present value of these cash flows? What is the present value at 18 percent? At 24 percent?

Basic
(Questions 1–28)

Year	Cash Flow
1	$ 900
2	600
3	1,100
4	1,480

2. **Present Value and Multiple Cash Flows.**   Investment X offers to pay you $4,000 per year for 9 years, whereas Investment Y offers to pay you $6,000 per year for 5 years. Which of these cash flow streams has the higher present value if the discount rate is 5 percent? If the discount rate is 22 percent?

3. **Future Value and Multiple Cash Flows.**   Rally, Inc., has identified an investment project with the following cash flows. If the discount rate is 8 percent, what is the future value of these cash flows in Year 4? What is the future value at a discount rate of 11 percent? At 24 percent?

Year	Cash Flow
1	$ 600
2	800
3	1,200
4	2,000

4. **Calculating Annuity Present Value.** An investment offers $4,500 per year for 15 years, with the first payment occurring 1 year from now. If the required return is 10 percent, what is the value of the investment? What would the value be if the payments occurred for 40 years? For 75 years? Forever?

5. **Calculating Annuity Cash Flows.** If you put up $15,000 today in exchange for a 7.5 percent, 12-year annuity, what will the annual cash flow be?

6. **Calculating Annuity Values.** Your company will generate $60,000 in revenue each year for the next nine years from a new information database. The computer system needed to set up the database costs $325,000. If you can borrow the money to buy the computer system at 8.25 percent annual interest, can you afford the new system?

7. **Calculating Annuity Values.** If you deposit $3,000 at the end of each of the next 20 years into an account paying 8.5 percent interest, how much money will you have in the account in 20 years? How much will you have if you make deposits for 40 years?

8. **Calculating Annuity Values.** You want to have $40,000 in your savings account seven years from now, and you're prepared to make equal annual deposits into the account at the end of each year. If the account pays 5.25 percent interest, what amount must you deposit each year?

9. **Calculating Annuity Values.** Bath's Bank offers you a $30,000, seven-year term loan at 9 percent annual interest. What will your annual loan payment be?

10. **Calculating Perpetuity Values.** Curly's Life Insurance Co. is trying to sell you an investment policy that will pay you and your heirs $20,000 per year forever. If the required return on this investment is 8 percent, how much will you pay for the policy?

11. **Calculating Perpetuity Values.** In the previous problem, suppose Curly's told you the policy costs $270,000. At what interest rate would this be a fair deal?

12. **Calculating EAR.** Find the EAR in each of the following cases:

Stated Rate (APR)	Number of Times Compounded	Effective Rate (EAR)
8%	Quarterly	
10	Monthly	
14	Daily	
18	Semiannually	

13. **Calculating APR.** Find the APR, or stated rate, in each of the following cases:

Stated Rate (APR)	Number of Times Compounded	Effective Rate (EAR)
	Semiannually	12%
	Monthly	18
	Weekly	7
	Daily	11

14. **Calculating EAR.**   First National Bank charges 13.1 percent compounded monthly on its business loans. First United Bank charges 13.4 percent compounded semiannually. As a potential borrower, which bank would you go to for a new loan?

15. **Calculating APR.**   Buckeye Credit Corp. wants to earn an effective annual return on its consumer loans of 17 percent per year. The bank uses daily compounding on its loans. What interest rate is the bank required by law to report to potential borrowers? Explain why this rate is misleading to an uninformed borrower.

16. **Calculating Future Values.**   What is the future value of $1,575 in 13 years assuming an interest rate of 10 percent compounded semiannually?

17. **Calculating Future Values.**   Bucher Credit Bank is offering 3.9 percent compounded daily on its savings accounts. If you deposit $6,000 today, how much will you have in the account in five years? In 10 years? In 20 years?

18. **Calculating Present Values.**   An investment will pay you $70,000 in six years. If the appropriate discount rate is 10 percent compounded daily, what is the present value?

19. **EAR versus APR.**   Ricky Ripov's Pawn Shop charges an interest rate of 25 percent per month on loans to its customers. Like all lenders, Ricky must report an APR to consumers. What rate should the shop report? What is the effective annual rate?

20. **Calculating Loan Payments.**   You want to buy a new sports coupe for $62,500, and the finance office at the dealership has quoted you an 8.2 percent APR loan for 60 months to buy the car. What will your monthly payments be? What is the effective annual rate on this loan?

21. **Calculating Number of Periods.**   One of your customers is delinquent on his accounts payable balance. You've mutually agreed to a repayment schedule of $400 per month. You will charge 1.3 percent per month interest on the overdue balance. If the current balance is $12,815, how long will it take for the account to be paid off?

22. **Calculating EAR.**   Friendly's Quick Loans, Inc., offers you "five for four, or I knock on your door." This means you get $4 today and repay $5 when you get your paycheck in one week (or else). What's the effective annual return Friendly's earns on this lending business? If you were brave enough to ask, what APR would Friendly's say you were paying?

23. **Valuing Perpetuities.**   Maybepay Life Insurance Co. is selling a perpetual annuity contract that pays $3,000 monthly. The contract currently sells for $175,000. What is the monthly return on this investment vehicle? What is the APR? The effective annual return?

24. **Calculating Annuity Future Values.**   You are to make monthly deposits of $250 into a retirement account that pays 11 percent interest compounded monthly. If your first deposit will be made one month from now, how large will your retirement account be in 30 years?

25. **Calculating Annuity Future Values.**   In the previous problem, suppose you make $3,000 annual deposits into the same retirement account. How large will your account balance be in 30 years?

26. **Calculating Annuity Present Values.**   Beginning three months from now, you want to be able to withdraw $2,000 each quarter from your bank account to cover college expenses over the next four years. If the account pays .75 percent interest per quarter, how much do you need to have in your bank account today to meet your expense needs over the next four years?

27. **Discounted Cash Flow Analysis.**   If the appropriate discount rate for the following cash flows is 10 percent, what is the present value of the cash flows?

Year	Cash Flow
1	$700
2	900
3	400
4	800

28. **Discounted Cash Flow Analysis.**   If the appropriate discount rate for the following cash flows is 7.83 percent per year, what is the present value of the cash flows?

Year	Cash Flow
1	$1,500
2	3,200
3	6,800
4	8,100

Intermediate
(Questions 29–56)

29. **Simple Interest versus Compound Interest.**   First Simple Bank pays 9 percent simple interest on its investment accounts. If First Complex Bank pays interest on its accounts compounded annually, what rate should the bank set if it wants to match First Simple Bank over an investment horizon of 10 years?

30. **Calculating Annuities Due.**   You want to buy a new sports car from Muscle Motors for $56,000. The contract is in the form of a 60-month annuity due at a 8.15 percent APR. What will your monthly payment be?

31. **Calculating Interest Expense.**   You receive a credit card application from Shady Banks Savings and Loan offering an introductory rate of 2.1 percent per year, compounded monthly for the first six months, increasing thereafter to 21 percent compounded monthly. Assuming you transfer the $6,000 balance from your existing credit card and make no subsequent payments, how much interest will you owe at the end of the first year?

32. **Calculating the Number of Periods.**   You are saving to buy a $150,000 house. There are two competing banks in your area, both offering certificates of deposit yielding 5 percent. How long will it take your initial $83,000 investment to reach the desired level at First Bank, which pays simple interest? How long at Second Bank, which compounds interest monthly?

33. **Calculating Future Values.**   You have an investment that will pay you 1.19 percent per month. How much will you have per dollar invested in one year? In two years?

34. **Calculating Annuity Interest Rates.**   Although you may know William Shakespeare from his classic literature, what is not well-known is that he was an astute investor. In 1604, when he was 40 and writing *King Lear,* Shakespeare grew worried about his eventual retirement. Afraid that he would become like King Lear in his retirement and beg hospitality from his children, he purchased grain "tithes," or shares in farm output, for 440 pounds. The tithes paid him 60 pounds per year for 31 years. Even though he died at the age of 52, his children received the remaining payments. What interest rate did the Bard of Avon receive on this investment?

35. Comparing Cash Flow Streams. You've just joined the investment banking firm of Dewey, Cheatum, and Howe. They've offered you two different salary arrangements. You can have $6,200 per month for the next two years, or you can have $4,900 per month for the next two years, along with a $30,000 signing bonus today. If the interest rate is 8 percent compounded monthly, which do you prefer?

36. Calculating Present Value of Annuities. Peter Lynchpin wants to sell you an investment contract that pays equal $18,000 amounts at the end of each of the next 20 years. If you require an effective annual return of 10 percent on this investment, how much will you pay for the contract today?

37. Calculating Rates of Return. You're trying to choose between two different investments, both of which have up-front costs of $50,000. Investment G returns $80,000 in six years. Investment H returns $140,000 in 13 years. Which of these investments has the higher return?

38. Present Value and Interest Rates. What is the relationship between the value of an annuity and the level of interest rates? Suppose you just bought a 10-year annuity of $6,000 per year at the current interest rate of 10 percent per year. What happens to the value of your investment if interest rates suddenly drop to 5 percent? What if interest rates suddenly rise to 15 percent?

39. Calculating the Number of Payments. You're prepared to make monthly payments of $140, beginning at the end of this month, into an account that pays 12 percent interest compounded monthly. How many payments will you have made when your account balance reaches $35,000?

40. Calculating Annuity Present Values. You want to borrow $60,000 from your local bank to buy a new sailboat. You can afford to make monthly payments of $1,300, but no more. Assuming monthly compounding, what is the highest rate you can afford on a 60-month APR loan?

41. Calculating Present Values. In the 1994 NBA draft, no one was surprised when the Milwaukee Bucks took Glenn "Big Dog" Robinson with the first pick. But Robinson wanted big bucks from the Bucks: a 13-year deal worth a total of $100 million. He had to settle for about $68 million over 10 years. His contract called for $2.9 million the first year, with annual raises of $870,000. So, how big a bite did Big Dog really take? Assume an 11 percent discount rate.

42. Calculating Present Values. In our previous question, we looked at the numbers for Big Dog's basketball contract. Now let's take a look at the terms for Shaquille "Shaq" O'Neal, the number one pick in 1992 who was drafted by the Orlando Magic. Shaquille signed a seven-year contract with estimated total payments of about $40 million. Although the precise terms were not disclosed, it was reported that Shaq would receive a salary of $3 million the first year, with raises of $900,000 each year thereafter. If the cash flows are discounted at the same 11 percent discount rate we used for Robinson, does the "Shaq Attack" result in the same kind of numbers? Did Robinson achieve his goal of being paid more than any other rookie in NBA history, including Shaq? Are the different contract lengths a factor? (Hint: Yes.)

43. EAR versus APR. You have just purchased a new warehouse. To finance the purchase, you've arranged for a 30-year mortgage loan for 80 percent of the $1,500,000 purchase price. The monthly payment on this loan will be $8,400. What is the APR on this loan? The EAR?

44. Annuity Values. You are planning your retirement in 10 years. You currently have $200,000 in a bond account and $400,000 in a stock account. You plan to add

$10,000 per year at the end of each of the next 10 years to your bond account. The stock account will earn an 11.5 percent return and the bond account will earn a 7.5 percent return. When you retire, you plan to withdraw an equal amount for each of the next 25 years at the end of each year and have nothing left. Additionally, when you retire you will transfer your money to an account that earns 6.75 percent. How much can you withdraw each year?

45. Discount Interest Loans. This question illustrates what is known as *discount interest.* Imagine you are discussing a loan with a somewhat unscrupulous lender. You want to borrow $12,000 for one year. The interest rate is 11 percent. You and the lender agree that the interest on the loan will be .11 × $12,000 = $1,320. So the lender deducts this interest amount from the loan up front and gives you $10,680. In this case, we say that the discount is $1,320. What's wrong here?

46. Calculating Annuities Due. As discussed in the text, an ordinary annuity assumes equal payments at the end of each period over the life of the annuity. An *annuity due* is the same thing except the payments occur at the beginning of each period instead. Thus, a three-year annual annuity due would have periodic payment cash flows occurring at Years 0, 1, and 2, whereas a three-year annual ordinary annuity would have periodic payment cash flows occurring at Years 1, 2, and 3.

    a. At a 13 percent annual discount rate, find the present value of a four-year ordinary annuity contract of $900 payments.

    b. Find the present value of the same contract if it is an annuity due.

47. Annuity and Perpetuity Values. Mary is going to receive a 30-year annuity of $6,000. Nancy is going to receive a perpetuity of $6,000. If the appropriate interest rate is 8 percent, how much more is Nancy's cash flow worth?

48. Calculating Present Values. A 5-year annuity of 10 $7,000 semiannual payments will begin 9 years from now, with the first payment coming 9.5 years from now. If the discount rate is 12 percent compounded semiannually, what is the value of this annuity five years from now? What is the value three years from now? What is the current value of the annuity?

49. Present Value and Multiple Cash Flows. What is the present value of $890 per year, at a discount rate of 9 percent, if the first payment is received 5 years from now and the last payment is received 20 years from now?

50. Variable Interest Rates. A 10-year annuity pays $1,300 per month, and payments are made at the end of each month. If the interest rate is 11 percent compounded monthly for the first four years, and 8 percent compounded monthly thereafter, what is the present value of the annuity?

51. Comparing Cash Flow Streams. You have your choice of two investment accounts. Investment A is a 10-year annuity that features end-of-month $1,600 payments and has an interest rate of 10 percent compounded monthly. Investment B is a 8 percent annually compounded lump-sum investment, also good for 10 years. How much money would you need to invest in B today for it to be worth as much as Investment A 10 years from now?

52. Calculating Present Value of a Perpetuity. Given an interest rate of 5.45 percent per year, what is the value at date $t = 9$ of a perpetual stream of $1,400 payments that begin at date $t = 15$?

53. Calculating EAR. A local finance company quotes a 13 percent interest rate on one-year loans. So, if you borrow $20,000, the interest for the year will be $2,600.

Because you must repay a total of $22,600 in one year, the finance company requires you to pay $22,600/12, or $1,833.33, per month over the next 12 months. Is this a 13 percent loan? What rate would legally have to be quoted? What is the effective annual rate?

54. **Calculating Future Values.**   If today is Year 0, what is the future value of the following cash flows five years from now? What is the future value 10 years from now? Assume a discount rate of 10.2 percent per year.

Year	Cash Flow
2	$25,000
3	45,000
5	65,000

55. **Amortization with Equal Payments.**   Prepare an amortization schedule for a three-year loan of $45,000. The interest rate is 11 percent per year, and the loan calls for equal annual payments. How much interest is paid in the third year? How much total interest is paid over the life of the loan?

56. **Amortization with Equal Principal Payments.**   Rework Problem 55 assuming that the loan agreement calls for a principal reduction of $15,000 every year instead of equal annual payments.

WHAT'S ON THE WEB?

5.1   **Annuity Future Value.**   The St. Louis Federal Reserve Board has files listing historical interest rates on their Web site www.stls.frb.org. Follow the link for "FRED II® (Federal Reserve Economic Data)." You will find listings for Moody's Seasoned Aaa Corporate Bond Yield and Moody's Seasoned Baa Corporate Bond Yield. (These rates are discussed in the next chapter.) If you invest $2,000 per year for the next 40 years at the most recent Aaa yield, how much will you have? What if you invest the same amount at the Baa yield?

5.2   **Loan Payments.**   Finding the time necessary until you pay off a loan is simple if you make equal payments each month. However, when paying off credit cards many individuals only make the minimum monthly payment, which is generally $10 or 2 percent to 3 percent of the balance, whichever is greater. You can find a credit card calculator at www.fincalc.com. You currently owe $10,000 on a credit card with a 17 percent interest rate and a minimum payment of $10 or 2 percent of your balance, whichever is greater. How soon will you pay off this debt if you make the minimum payment each month? How much total interest will you pay?

5.3   **Annuity Payments.**   Find the retirement calculator at www.moneychimp.com to answer the following question: Suppose you have $1,500,000 when you retire and want to withdraw an equal amount each year for the next 30 years. How much can you withdraw each year if you earn 7 percent? What if you can earn 9 percent?

5.4   **Annuity Payments.**   The St. Louis Federal Reserve Board has files listing historical interest rates on their Web site www.stls.frb.org. Follow the link for "FRED II® (Federal Reserve Economic Data)." You will find a listing for the

Bank Prime Loan Rate. The file lists the monthly prime rates since January 1949 (1949.01). What is the most recent prime rate? What is the highest prime rate over this period? If you buy a house for $150,000 at the current prime rate on a 30-year mortgage with monthly payments, how much are your payments? If you had purchased the house at the same price when the prime rate was at its highest, what would your monthly payments have been?

5.5   **Loan Amortization.**   Bankrate.com, located at www.bankrate.com, has a financial calculator that will prepare an amortization table based on your inputs. First, find the APR quoted on the Web site for a 30-year fixed rate mortgage. You want to buy a home for $200,000 on a 30-year mortgage with monthly payments at the rate quoted on the site. What percentage of your first month's payment is principal? What percentage of you last month's payment is principal? What is the total interest paid on the loan?

S&S AIR'S MORTGAGE

Mark Sexton and Todd Story, the owners of S&S Air, Inc., were impressed by the work Chris had done on financial planning. Using Chris's analysis, and looking at the demand for light aircraft, they have decided that their existing fabrication equipment is sufficient, but it is time to acquire a bigger manufacturing facility. Mark and Todd have identified a suitable structure that is currently for sale, and they believe they can buy and refurbish it for about $20 million. Mark, Todd, and Chris are now ready to meet with Christie Vaughan, the loan officer for First United National Bank. The meeting is to discuss the mortgage options available to the company to finance the new facility.

Christie begins the meeting by discussing a 30-year mortgage. The loan would be repaid in equal monthly installments. Because of the previous relationship between S&S Air and the bank, there would be no closing costs for the loan. Christie states that the APR of the loan would be 6.2 percent. Todd asks if a shorter mortgage loan is available. Christie says that the bank does have a 20-year mortgage available at the same APR.

Mark decides to ask Christie about a "smart loan" he discussed with a mortgage broker when he was refinancing his home loan. A smart loan works as follows: Every two weeks a mortgage payment is made that is exactly one-half of the traditional monthly mortgage payment. Christie informs him that the bank does have smart loans. The APR of the smart loan would be the same as the APR of the traditional loan. Mark nods his head. He then states this is the best mortgage option available to the company since it saves interest payments.

Christie agrees with Mark, but then suggests that a bullet loan, or balloon payment, would result in the greatest interest savings. At Todd's prompting she goes on to explain a bullet loan. The monthly payments of a bullet loan would be calculated using a 30-year traditional mortgage. In this case, there would be a 5-year bullet. This would mean that the company would make the mortgage payments for the traditional 30-year mortgage for the first five years, but immediately after the company makes the 60th payment, the bullet payment would be due. The bullet payment is the remaining principal of the loan. Chris then asks how the bullet payment is calculated. Christie tells him that the remaining principal can be calculated using an amortization table, but it is also the present value of the remaining 25 years of mortgage payments for the 30-year mortgage.

Todd has also heard of an interest-only loan and asks if this loan is available and what the terms would be. Christie says that the bank offers an interest-only loan with a term of 10 years and an APR of 3.5 percent. She goes on to further explain the terms. The company would be responsible for making interest payments each month on the amount borrowed. No principal payments are required. At the end of the 10-year term, the company would repay the $20 million. However, the company can make principal payments at any time. The principle payments would work just like those on a traditional mortgage. Principal payments would reduce the principal of the loan and reduce the interest due on the next payment.

Mark and Todd are satisfied with Christie's answers, but they are still unsure of which loan they should choose. They have asked Chris to answer the following questions to help them choose the correct mortgage.

QUESTIONS

1. What are the monthly payments for a 30-year traditional mortgage? What are the payments for a 20-year traditional mortgage?

2. Prepare an amortization table for the first six months of the traditional 30-year mortgage. How much of the first payment goes toward principal?

3. How long would it take for S&S Air to pay off the smart loan assuming 30-year traditional mortgage payments? Why is this shorter than the time needed to pay off the traditional mortgage? How much interest would the company save?

4. Assume S&S Air takes out a bullet loan under the terms described. What are the payments on the loan?

5. What are the payments for the interest-only loan?

6. Which mortgage is the best for the company? Are there any potential risks in this action?

In January 2005 Sharp Corp., the Japanese electronics company, announced plans to build a $1.5 billion plant to manufacture eighth-generation glass sheets for liquid-crystal display (LCD) panels. The plant would manufacture glass sheets big enough to cut into eight 40-inch or six 50-inch television screens. The company had just opened a sixth-generation plant one year earlier, which at the time was the newest generation plant. And the success of the eighth-generation plant was not guaranteed. Sharp still faced stiff competition from companies producing large screen plasma televisions.

8   Net Present Value and Other Investment Criteria

Sharp's announcement offers an example of a capital budgeting decision. An expansion such as this one, with a $1.5 billion price tag, is obviously a major undertaking, and the potential risks and rewards must be carefully weighed. In this chapter, we discuss the basic tools used in making such decisions.

This chapter introduces you to the practice of capital budgeting. Back in Chapter 1 we saw that increasing the value of the stock in a company is the goal of financial management. Thus, what we need to learn is how to tell whether a particular investment will achieve that or not. This chapter considers a variety of techniques that are actually used in practice. More importantly, it shows how many of these techniques can be misleading, and it explains why the net present value approach is the right one.

AFTER STUDYING THIS CHAPTER, YOU SHOULD HAVE A GOOD UNDERSTANDING OF:

■ The payback rule and some of its shortcomings.

■ Accounting rates of return and some of the problems with them.

■ The internal rate of return criterion and its strengths and weaknesses.

■ Why the net present value criterion is the best way to evaluate proposed investments.

In Chapter 1, we identified the three key areas of concern to the financial manager. The first of these was the following: What long-term investments should we make? We called this the *capital budgeting decision*. In this chapter, we begin to deal with the issues that arise in answering this question.

The process of allocating, or budgeting, capital is usually more involved than just deciding whether or not to buy a particular fixed asset. We will frequently face broader issues like whether or not we should launch a new product or enter a new market. Decisions such as these will determine the nature of a firm's operations and products for years to come, primarily because fixed asset investments are generally long-lived and not easily reversed once they are made.

For these reasons, the capital budgeting question is probably the most important issue in corporate finance. How a firm chooses to finance its operations (the capital structure question) and how a firm manages its short-term operating activities (the working capital question) are certainly issues of concern, but it is the fixed assets that define the business of the firm. Airlines, for example, are airlines because they operate airplanes, regardless of how they finance them.

Any firm possesses a huge number of possible investments. Each possible investment is an option available to the firm. Some options are valuable and some are not. The essence of successful financial management, of course, is learning to identify which are which. With this in mind, our goal in this chapter is to introduce you to the techniques used to analyze potential business ventures to decide which are worth undertaking.

We present and compare several different procedures used in practice. Our primary goal is to acquaint you with the advantages and disadvantages of the various approaches. As we shall see, the most important concept in this area is the idea of net present value. We consider this next.

8.1 | NET PRESENT VALUE

In Chapter 1, we argued that the goal of financial management is to create value for the stockholders. The financial manager must therefore examine a potential investment in light of its likely effect on the price of the firm's shares. In this section, we describe a widely used procedure for doing this, the net present value approach.

The Basic Idea

An investment is worth undertaking if it creates value for its owners. In the most general sense, we create value by identifying an investment worth more in the marketplace than it costs us to acquire. How can something be worth more than it costs? It's a case of the whole being worth more than the cost of the parts.

For example, suppose you buy a run-down house for $25,000 and spend another $25,000 on painters, plumbers, and so on to get it fixed up. Your total investment is $50,000. When the work is completed, you place the house back on the market and find that it's worth $60,000. The market value ($60,000) exceeds the cost ($50,000) by $10,000. What you have done here is to act as a manager and bring together some fixed assets (a house), some labor (plumbers, carpenters, and others), and some materials (carpeting, paint, and so on). The net result is that you have created $10,000 in value. Put another way, this $10,000 is the *value added* by management.

With our house example, it turned out *after the fact* that $10,000 in value was created. Things thus worked out very nicely. The real challenge, of course, would have been to somehow identify *ahead of time* whether or not investing the necessary $50,000 was a good idea in the first place. This is what capital budgeting is all about, namely, trying to determine whether a proposed investment or project will be worth more than it costs once it is in place.

For reasons that will be obvious in a moment, the difference between an investment's market value and its cost is called the **net present value** of the investment, abbreviated **NPV**. In other words, net present value is a measure of how much value is created or added today by undertaking an investment. Given our goal of creating value for the stockholders, the capital budgeting process can be viewed as a search for investments with positive net present values.

With our run-down house, you can probably imagine how we would go about making the capital budgeting decision. We would first look at what comparable, fixed-up properties were selling for in the market. We would then get estimates of the cost of buying a particular property, fixing it up, and bringing it to market. At this point, we have an estimated total cost and an estimated market value. If the difference is positive, then this investment is worth undertaking because it has a positive estimated net present value. There is risk, of course, because there is no guarantee that our estimates will turn out to be correct.

As our example illustrates, investment decisions are greatly simplified when there is a market for assets similar to the investment we are considering. Capital budgeting becomes much more difficult when we cannot observe the market price for at least roughly comparable investments. The reason is that we are then faced with the problem of estimating the value of an investment using only indirect market information. Unfortunately, this is precisely the situation the financial manager usually encounters. We examine this issue next.

net present value (NPV)
The difference between an investment's market value and its cost.

Estimating Net Present Value

Imagine we are thinking of starting a business to produce and sell a new product, say, organic fertilizer. We can estimate the start-up costs with reasonable accuracy because we know what we will need to buy to begin production. Would this be a good investment? Based on our discussion, you know that the answer depends on whether or not the value of the new business exceeds the cost of starting it. In other words, does this investment have a positive NPV?

This problem is much more difficult than our "fixer-upper" house example, because entire fertilizer companies are not routinely bought and sold in the marketplace; so it is essentially impossible to observe the market value of a similar investment. As a result, we must somehow estimate this value by other means.

Based on our work in Chapters 4 and 5, you may be able to guess how we will go about estimating the value of our fertilizer business. We will first try to estimate the future cash flows we expect the new business to produce. We will then apply our basic discounted cash flow procedure to estimate the present value of those cash flows. Once we have this estimate, we then estimate NPV as the difference between the present value of the future cash flows and the cost of the investment. As we mentioned in Chapter 5, this procedure is often called **discounted cash flow**, or **DCF, valuation**.

discounted cash flow (DCF) valuation
The process of valuing an investment by discounting its future cash flows.

To see how we might go about estimating NPV, suppose we believe the cash revenues from our fertilizer business will be $20,000 per year, assuming everything goes as expected. Cash costs (including taxes) will be $14,000 per year. We will wind down the business in eight years. The plant, property, and equipment will be worth $2,000 as salvage at that time. The project costs $30,000 to launch. We use a 15 percent discount rate on new projects such as this one. Is this a good investment? If there are 1,000 shares of stock outstanding, what will be the effect on the price per share from taking the investment?

From a purely mechanical perspective, we need to calculate the present value of the future cash flows at 15 percent. The net cash inflow will be $20,000 cash income less $14,000 in costs per year for eight years. These cash flows are illustrated in Figure 8.1.

FIGURE 8.1

Project cash flows ($000)

Time (years)	0	1	2	3	4	5	6	7	8
Initial cost	–$30								
Inflows		$20	$20	$20	$20	$20	$20	$20	$20
Outflows		– 14	– 14	– 14	– 14	– 14	– 14	– 14	– 14
Net inflow		$ 6	$ 6	$ 6	$ 6	$ 6	$ 6	$ 6	$ 6
Salvage									2
Net cash flow	–$30	$ 6	$ 6	$ 6	$ 6	$ 6	$ 6	$ 6	$ 8

Find out more about capital budgeting for small businesses at **www. missouribusiness.net.**

As Figure 8.1 suggests, we effectively have an eight-year annuity of $20,000 − 14,000 = $6,000 per year along with a single lump-sum inflow of $2,000 in eight years. Calculating the present value of the future cash flows thus comes down to the same type of problem we considered in Chapter 5. The total present value is:

$$\text{Present value} = \$6,000 \times (1 - 1/1.15^8)/.15 + 2,000/1.15^8$$
$$= \$6,000 \times 4.4873 + 2,000/3.0590$$
$$= \$26,924 + 654$$
$$= \$27,578$$

When we compare this to the $30,000 estimated cost, the NPV is:

$$\text{NPV} = -\$30,000 + 27,578 = -\$2,422$$

Therefore, this is *not* a good investment. Based on our estimates, taking it would *decrease* the total value of the stock by $2,422. With 1,000 shares outstanding, our best estimate of the impact of taking this project is a loss of value of $2,422/1,000 = $2.422 per share.

Our fertilizer example illustrates how NPV estimates can be used to determine whether or not an investment is desirable. From our example, notice that if the NPV is negative, the effect on share value will be unfavorable. If the NPV were positive, the effect would be favorable. As a consequence, all we need to know about a particular proposal for the purpose of making an accept-reject decision is whether the NPV is positive or negative.

Given that the goal of financial management is to increase share value, our discussion in this section leads us to the *net present value rule:*

An investment should be accepted if the net present value is positive and rejected if it is negative.

In the unlikely event that the net present value turned out to be exactly zero, we would be indifferent between taking the investment and not taking it.

Two comments about our example are in order. First and foremost, it is not the rather mechanical process of discounting the cash flows that is important. Once we have the cash flows and the appropriate discount rate, the required calculations are fairly straightforward. The task of coming up with the cash flows and the discount rate in the first place is much more challenging. We will have much more to say about this in our next chapter. For the remainder of this chapter, we take it as given that we have estimates of the cash revenues and costs and, where needed, an appropriate discount rate.

The second thing to keep in mind about our example is that the −$2,422 NPV is an estimate. Like any estimate, it can be high or low. The only way to find out the true NPV would be to place the investment up for sale and see what we could get for it. We generally won't be doing this, so it is important that our estimates be reliable. Once again, we will have more to say about this later. For the rest of this chapter, we will assume that the estimates are accurate.

accept if NPV is +

Using the NPV Rule   EXAMPLE 8.1

Suppose we are asked to decide whether or not a new consumer product should be launched. Based on projected sales and costs, we expect that the cash flows over the five-year life of the project will be $2,000 in the first two years, $4,000 in the next two, and $5,000 in the last year. It will cost about $10,000 to begin production. We use a 10 percent discount rate to evaluate new products. What should we do here?

Given the cash flows and discount rate, we can calculate the total value of the product by discounting the cash flows back to the present:

Present value = $2,000/1.1 + 2,000/1.1^2 + 4,000/1.1^3 + 4,000/1.1^4 + 5,000/1.1^5
   = $1,818 + 1,653 + 3,005 + 2,732 + 3,105
   = $12,313

The present value of the expected cash flows is $12,313, but the cost of getting those cash flows is only $10,000, so the NPV is $12,313 − 10,000 = $2,313. This is positive; so, based on the net present value rule, we should take on the project.

You can get a freeware NPV calculator at **www. wheatworks.com.**

Calculating NPVs with a Spreadsheet   SPREADSHEET STRATEGIES

Spreadsheets and financial calculators are commonly used to calculate NPVs. The procedures used by various financial calculators are too different for us to illustrate here, so we will focus on using a spreadsheet (financial calculators are covered in Appendix D). Examining the use of spreadsheets in this context also allows us to issue an important warning. Let's rework Example 8.1:

	A	B	C	D	E	F	G	H
1								
2			Using a spreadsheet to calculate net present values					
3								
4	From Example 8.1, the project's cost is $10,000. The cash flows are $2,000 per year for the first two							
5	years, $4,000 per year for the next two, and $5,000 in the last year. The discount rate is							
6	10 percent; what's the NPV?							
7								
8		Year	Cash flow					
9		0	−$10,000	Discount rate =		10%		
10		1	2,000					
11		2	2,000		NPV =	$2,102.72	(*wrong* answer)	
12		3	4,000		NPV =	$2,312.99	(*right* answer)	
13		4	4,000					
14		5	5,000					
15								
16	The formula entered in cell F11 is = NPV(F9,C9:C14). This gives the wrong answer because the							
17	NPV function actually calculates present values, not net present values.							
18								
19	The formula entered in cell F12 is = NPV(F9,C10:C14) + C9. This gives the right answer because the							
20	NPV function is used to calculate the present value of the cash flows and then the initial cost is							
21	subtracted to calculate the answer. Notice that we added cell C9 because it is already negative.							

As we have seen in this section, estimating NPV is one way of assessing the profitability of a proposed investment. It is certainly not the only way profitability is assessed, and we now turn to some alternatives. As we will see, when compared to NPV, each of the ways of assessing profitability that we examine is flawed in some key way; so, NPV is the preferred approach in principle, if not always in practice.

In our nearby *Spreadsheet Strategies* box, we rework Example 8.1. Notice that we have provided two answers. By comparing the answers to that found in Example 8.1, we see that the first answer is wrong even though we used the spreadsheet's NPV formula. What happened is that the "NPV" function in our spreadsheet is actually a PV function; unfortunately, one of the original spreadsheet programs many years ago got the definition wrong, and subsequent spreadsheets have copied it! Our second answer shows how to use the formula properly.

The example here illustrates the danger of blindly using calculators or computers without understanding what is going on; we shudder to think of how many capital budgeting decisions in the real world are based on incorrect use of this particular function. We will see another example of something that can go wrong with a spreadsheet later in the chapter.

CONCEPT QUESTIONS

8.1a   What is the net present value rule?

8.1b   If we say an investment has an NPV of $1,000, what exactly do we mean?

8.2 | THE PAYBACK RULE

It is very common in practice to talk of the payback on a proposed investment. Loosely, the *payback* is the length of time it takes to recover our initial investment, or "get our bait back." Because this idea is widely understood and used, we will examine it in some detail.

Defining the Rule

We can illustrate how to calculate a payback with an example. Figure 8.2 below shows the cash flows from a proposed investment. How many years do we have to wait until the accumulated cash flows from this investment equal or exceed the cost of the investment? As Figure 8.2 indicates, the initial investment is $50,000. After the first year, the firm has recovered $30,000, leaving $20,000 outstanding. The cash flow in the second year is exactly $20,000, so this investment "pays for itself" in exactly two years. Put another way, the **payback period** (or just payback) is two years. If we require a payback of, say, three years or less, then this investment is acceptable. This illustrates the *payback period rule:*

payback period
The amount of time required for an investment to generate cash flows sufficient to recover its initial cost.

> Based on the payback rule, an investment is acceptable if its calculated payback period is less than some prespecified number of years.

In our example, the payback works out to be exactly two years. This won't usually happen, of course. When the numbers don't work out exactly, it is customary to work with

Net project cash flows

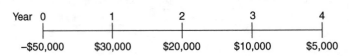

Year	0	1	2	3	4
	−$50,000	$30,000	$20,000	$10,000	$5,000

fractional years. For example, suppose the initial investment is $60,000, and the cash flows are $20,000 in the first year and $90,000 in the second. The cash flows over the first two years are $110,000, so the project obviously pays back sometime in the second year. After the first year, the project has paid back $20,000, leaving $40,000 to be recovered. To figure out the fractional year, note that this $40,000 is $40,000/90,000 = 4/9 of the second year's cash flow. Assuming that the $90,000 cash flow is paid uniformly throughout the year, the payback would thus be 1⁴⁄₉ years.

Calculating Payback   EXAMPLE 8.2

The projected cash flows from a proposed investment are:

Year	Cash Flow
1	$100
2	200
3	500

This project costs $500. What is the payback period for this investment?

The initial cost is $500. After the first two years, the cash flows total $300. After the third year, the total cash flow is $800, so the project pays back sometime between the end of Year 2 and the end of Year 3. Since the accumulated cash flows for the first two years are $300, we need to recover $200 in the third year. The third-year cash flow is $500, so we will have to wait $200/500 = .40 year to do this. The payback period is thus 2.4 years, or about two years and five months.

Now that we know how to calculate the payback period on an investment, using the payback period rule for making decisions is straightforward. A particular cutoff time is selected, say, two years, and all investment projects that have payback periods of two years or less are accepted, and all of those that pay back in more than two years are rejected.

Table 8.1 illustrates cash flows for five different projects. The figures shown as the Year 0 cash flows are the cost of the investment. We examine these to indicate some peculiarities that can, in principle, arise with payback periods.

The payback for the first project, A, is easily calculated. The sum of the cash flows for the first two years is $70, leaving us with $100 − 70 = $30 to go. Since the cash flow in the third year is $50, the payback occurs sometime in that year. When we compare the $30 we need to the $50 that will be coming in, we get $30/50 = .60; so, payback will occur 60 percent of the way into the year. The payback period is thus 2.6 years.

Year	A	B	C	D	E
0	−$100	−$200	−$200	−$200	−$ 50
1	30	40	40	100	100
2	40	20	20	100	− 50,000,000
3	50	10	10	− 200	
4	60		130	200	

TABLE 8.1

Expected cash flows for Projects A through E

Project B's payback is also easy to calculate: It *never* pays back because the cash flows never total up to the original investment. Project C has a payback of exactly four years because it supplies the $130 that B is missing in Year 4. Project D is a little strange. Because of the negative cash flow in Year 3, you can easily verify that it has two different payback periods, two years and four years. Which of these is correct? Both of them; the way the payback period is calculated doesn't guarantee a single answer. Finally, Project E is obviously unrealistic, but it does pay back in six months, thereby illustrating the point that a rapid payback does not guarantee a good investment.

Analyzing the Rule

When compared to the NPV rule, the payback period rule has some rather severe shortcomings. First, the payback period is calculated by simply adding up the future cash flows. There is no discounting involved, so the time value of money is completely ignored. The payback rule also fails to consider risk differences. The payback would be calculated the same way for both very risky and very safe projects.

Perhaps the biggest problem with the payback period rule is coming up with the right cutoff period, because we don't really have an objective basis for choosing a particular number. Put another way, there is no economic rationale for looking at payback in the first place, so we have no guide as to how to pick the cutoff. As a result, we end up using a number that is arbitrarily chosen.

Suppose we have somehow decided on an appropriate payback period, say two years or less. As we have seen, the payback period rule ignores the time value of money for the first two years. More seriously, cash flows after the second year are ignored entirely. To see this, consider the two investments, Long and Short, in Table 8.2. Both projects cost $250. Based on our discussion, the payback on Long is $2 + \$50/100 = 2.5$ years, and the payback on Short is $1 + \$150/200 = 1.75$ years. With a cutoff of two years, Short is acceptable and Long is not.

Is the payback period rule giving us the right decisions? Maybe not. Suppose again that we require a 15 percent return on this type of investment. We can calculate the NPV for these two investments as:

$$\text{NPV(Short)} = -\$250 + 100/1.15 + 200/1.15^2 = -\$11.81$$
$$\text{NPV(Long)} = -\$250 + 100 \times (1 - 1/1.15^4)/.15 = \$35.50$$

Now we have a problem. The NPV of the shorter-term investment is actually negative, meaning that taking it diminishes the value of the shareholders' equity. The opposite is true for the longer-term investment—it increases share value.

Our example illustrates two primary shortcomings of the payback period rule. First, by ignoring time value, we may be led to take investments (like Short) that actually are worth less than they cost. Second, by ignoring cash flows beyond the cutoff, we may be led to reject profitable long-term investments (like Long). More generally, using a payback period rule will tend to bias us towards shorter-term investments.

TABLE 8.2		
Investment projected cash flows		

Year	Long	Short
0	−$250	−$250
1	100	100
2	100	200
3	100	0
4	100	0

Redeeming Qualities of the Rule

Despite its shortcomings, the payback period rule is often used by large and sophisticated companies when they are making relatively minor decisions. There are several reasons for this. The primary reason is that many decisions simply do not warrant detailed analysis because the cost of the analysis would exceed the possible loss from a mistake. As a practical matter, an investment that pays back rapidly and has benefits extending beyond the cutoff period probably has a positive NPV.

Small investment decisions are made by the hundreds every day in large organizations. Moreover, they are made at all levels. As a result, it would not be uncommon for a corporation to require, for example, a two-year payback on all investments of less than $10,000. Investments larger than this are subjected to greater scrutiny. The requirement of a two-year payback is not perfect for reasons we have seen, but it does exercise some control over expenditures and thus has the effect of limiting possible losses.

In addition to its simplicity, the payback rule has two other positive features. First, because it is biased towards short-term projects, it is biased towards liquidity. In other words, a payback rule tends to favor investments that free up cash for other uses more quickly. This could be very important for a small business; it would be less so for a large corporation. Second, the cash flows that are expected to occur later in a project's life are probably more uncertain. Arguably, a payback period rule adjusts for the extra riskiness of later cash flows, but it does so in a rather draconian fashion—by ignoring them altogether.

We should note here that some of the apparent simplicity of the payback rule is an illusion. The reason is that we still must come up with the cash flows first, and, as we discuss above, this is not at all easy to do. Thus, it would probably be more accurate to say that the *concept* of a payback period is both intuitive and easy to understand.

Summary of the Rule

To summarize, the payback period is a kind of "break-even" measure. Because time value is ignored, you can think of the payback period as the length of time it takes to break even in an accounting sense, but not in an economic sense. The biggest drawback to the payback period rule is that it doesn't ask the right question. The relevant issue is the impact an investment will have on the value of our stock, not how long it takes to recover the initial investment.

Nevertheless, because it is so simple, companies often use it as a screen for dealing with the myriad of minor investment decisions they have to make. There is certainly nothing wrong with this practice. Like any simple rule of thumb, there will be some errors in using it, but it wouldn't have survived all this time if it weren't useful. Now that you understand the rule, you can be on the alert for those circumstances under which it might lead to problems. To help you remember, the following table lists the pros and cons of the payback period rule.

Advantages and Disadvantages of the Payback Period Rule	
Advantages	**Disadvantages**
1. Easy to understand.	1. Ignores the time value of money.
2. Adjusts for uncertainty of later cash flows.	2. Requires an arbitrary cutoff point.
3. Biased towards liquidity.	3. Ignores cash flows beyond the cutoff date.
	4. Biased against long-term projects, such as research and development, and new projects.

8.3 | THE AVERAGE ACCOUNTING RETURN

average accounting return (AAR)

An investment's average net income divided by its average book value.

Another attractive, but flawed, approach to making capital budgeting decisions involves the **average accounting return (AAR)**. There are many different definitions of the AAR. However, in one form or another, the AAR is always defined as:

$$\frac{\text{Some measure of average accounting profit}}{\text{Some measure of average accounting value}}$$

The specific definition we will use is:

$$\frac{\text{Average net income}}{\text{Average book value}}$$

To see how we might calculate this number, suppose we are deciding whether or not to open a store in a new shopping mall. The required investment in improvements is $500,000. The store would have a five-year life because everything reverts to the mall owners after that time. The required investment would be 100 percent depreciated (straight-line) over five years, so the depreciation would be $500,000/5 = $100,000 per year. The tax rate is 25 percent. Table 8.3 contains the projected revenues and expenses. Based on these figures, net income in each year is also shown.

To calculate the average book value for this investment, we note that we started out with a book value of $500,000 (the initial cost) and ended up at $0. The average book value during the life of the investment is thus ($500,000 + 0)/2 = $250,000. As long as we use straight-line depreciation and a zero salvage value, the average investment will always be one-half of the initial investment.[1]

Looking at Table 8.3, we see that net income is $100,000 in the first year, $150,000 in the second year, $50,000 in the third year, $0 in Year 4, and −$50,000 in Year 5. The average net income, then, is:

$$[\$100,000 + 150,000 + 50,000 + 0 + (-50,000)]/5 = \$50,000$$

The average accounting return is:

$$\text{AAR} = \frac{\text{Average net income}}{\text{Average book value}} = \frac{\$50,000}{250,000} = 20\%$$

If the firm has a target AAR less than 20 percent, then this investment is acceptable; otherwise, it is not. The *average accounting return rule* is thus:

---

[1]We could, of course, calculate the average of the six book values directly. In thousands, we would have ($500 + 400 + 300 + 200 + 100 + 0)/6 = $250.

	Year 1	Year 2	Year 3	Year 4	Year 5
Revenue	$433,333	$450,000	$266,667	$200,000	$133,333
Expenses	200,000	150,000	100,000	100,000	100,000
Earnings before depreciation	$233,333	$300,000	$166,667	$100,000	$ 33,333
Depreciation	100,000	100,000	100,000	100,000	100,000
Earnings before taxes	$133,333	$200,000	$ 66,667	$ 0	−$ 66,667
Taxes (25%)	33,333	50,000	16,667	0	− 16,667
Net income	$100,000	$150,000	$ 50,000	$ 0	−$ 50,000

TABLE 8.3

Projected yearly revenue and costs for average accounting return

$$\text{Average net income} = \frac{(\$100,000 + \$150,000 + \$50,000 + 0 - 50,000)}{5} = \$50,000$$

$$\text{Average book value} = \frac{\$500,000 + 0}{2} = \$250,000$$

> Based on the average accounting return rule, a project is acceptable if its average accounting return exceeds a target average accounting return.

As we will see next, this rule has a number of problems.

You should recognize the chief drawback to the AAR immediately. Above all else, the AAR is not a rate of return in any meaningful economic sense. Instead, it is the ratio of two accounting numbers, and it is not comparable to the returns offered, for example, in financial markets.[2]

One of the reasons the AAR is not a true rate of return is that it ignores time value. When we average figures that occur at different times, we are treating the near future and the more distant future the same way. There was no discounting involved when we computed the average net income, for example.

The second problem with the AAR is similar to the problem we had with the payback period rule concerning the lack of an objective cutoff period. Since a calculated AAR is really not comparable to a market return, the target AAR must somehow be specified. There is no generally agreed-upon way to do this. One way of doing it is to calculate the AAR for the firm as a whole and use this as a benchmark, but there are lots of other ways as well.

The third, and perhaps worst, flaw in the AAR is that it doesn't even look at the right things. Instead of cash flow and market value, it uses net income and book value. These are both poor substitutes. As a result, an AAR doesn't tell us what the effect on share price will be from taking an investment, so it doesn't tell us what we really want to know.

Does the AAR have any redeeming features? About the only one is that it almost always can be computed. The reason is that accounting information will almost always be available, both for the project under consideration and for the firm as a whole. We hasten to add that once the accounting information is available, we can always convert it to cash flows, so even this is not a particularly important fact. The AAR is summarized in the table that follows.

---

[2]The AAR is closely related to the return on assets, or ROA, discussed in Chapter 3. In practice, the AAR is sometimes computed by first calculating the ROA for each year and then averaging the results. This produces a number that is similar, but not identical, to the one we computed.

Advantages and Disadvantages of the Average Accounting Return	
Advantages	**Disadvantages**
1. Easy to calculate.	1. Not a true rate of return; time value of money is ignored.
2. Needed information will usually be available.	2. Uses an arbitrary benchmark cutoff rate.
	3. Based on accounting net income and book values, not cash flows and market values.

CONCEPT QUESTIONS

8.3a   What is an average accounting rate of return, or AAR?

8.3b   What are the weaknesses of the AAR rule?

8.4 | THE INTERNAL RATE OF RETURN

We now come to the most important alternative to NPV, the **internal rate of return**, universally known as the **IRR**. As we will see, the IRR is closely related to NPV. With the IRR, we try to find a single rate of return that summarizes the merits of a project. Furthermore, we want this rate to be an "internal" rate in the sense that it only depends on the cash flows of a particular investment, not on rates offered elsewhere.

To illustrate the idea behind the IRR, consider a project that costs $100 today and pays $110 in one year. Suppose you were asked, "What is the return on this investment?" What would you say? It seems both natural and obvious to say that the return is 10 percent because, for every dollar we put in, we get $1.10 back. In fact, as we will see in a moment, 10 percent is the internal rate of return, or IRR, on this investment.

internal rate of return (IRR)

The discount rate that makes the NPV of an investment zero.

Is this project with its 10 percent IRR a good investment? Once again, it would seem apparent that this is a good investment only if our required return is less than 10 percent. This intuition is also correct and illustrates the *IRR rule:*

> Based on the IRR rule, an investment is acceptable if the IRR exceeds the required return. It should be rejected otherwise.

Imagine that we wanted to calculate the NPV for our simple investment. At a discount rate of R, the NPV is:

$$NPV = -\$100 + 110/(1 + R)$$

Now, suppose we didn't know the discount rate. This presents a problem, but we could still ask how high the discount rate would have to be before this project was unacceptable. We know that we are indifferent between taking and not taking this investment when its NPV is just equal to zero. In other words, this investment is *economically* a break-even proposition when the NPV is zero because value is neither created nor destroyed. To find the break-even discount rate, we set NPV equal to zero and solve for R:

$$NPV = 0 = -\$100 + 110/(1 + R)$$
$$\$100 = \$110/(1 + R)$$
$$1 + R = \$110/100 = 1.10$$
$$R = 10\%$$

This 10 percent is what we already have called the return on this investment. What we have now illustrated is that the internal rate of return on an investment (or just "return" for short) is the discount rate that makes the NPV equal to zero. This is an important observation, so it bears repeating:

> The IRR on an investment is the required return that results in a zero NPV when it is used as the discount rate.

The fact that the IRR is simply the discount rate that makes the NPV equal to zero is important because it tells us how to calculate the returns on more complicated investments. As we have seen, finding the IRR turns out to be relatively easy for a single-period investment. However, suppose you were now looking at an investment with the cash flows shown in Figure 8.3. As illustrated, this investment costs $100 and has a cash flow of $60 per year for two years, so it's only slightly more complicated than our single-period example. However, if you were asked for the return on this investment, what would you say? There doesn't seem to be any obvious answer (at least to us). However, based on what we now know, we can set the NPV equal to zero and solve for the discount rate:

$$NPV = 0 = -\$100 + 60/(1 + IRR) + 60/(1 + IRR)^2$$

Unfortunately, the only way to find the IRR in general is by trial and error, either by hand or by calculator. This is precisely the same problem that came up in Chapter 5 when we found the unknown rate for an annuity and in Chapter 6 when we found the yield to maturity on a bond. In fact, we now see that, in both of those cases, we were finding an IRR.

In this particular case, the cash flows form a two-period, $60 annuity. To find the unknown rate, we can try some different rates until we get the answer. If we were to start with a 0 percent rate, the NPV would obviously be $120 − 100 = $20. At a 10 percent discount rate, we would have:

$$NPV = -\$100 + 60/1.1 + 60/1.1^2 = \$4.13$$

Now, we're getting close. We can summarize these and some other possibilities as shown in Table 8.4. From our calculations, the NPV appears to be zero between 10 percent and 15 percent, so the IRR is somewhere in that range. With a little more effort, we can find that the IRR is about 13.1 percent. So, if our required return is less than 13.1 percent, we would take this investment. If our required return exceeds 13.1 percent, we would reject it.

By now, you have probably noticed that the IRR rule and the NPV rule appear to be quite similar. In fact, the IRR is sometimes simply called the *discounted cash flow*, or *DCF*, *return*. The easiest way to illustrate the relationship between NPV and IRR is to plot the numbers we calculated in Table 8.4. We put the different NPVs on the vertical axis, or

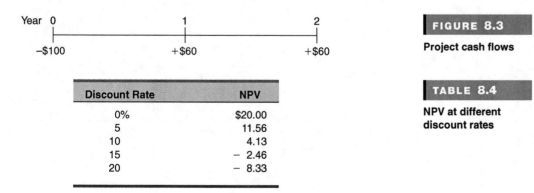

Year	0	1	2
	−$100	+$60	+$60

FIGURE 8.3

Project cash flows

Discount Rate	NPV
0%	$20.00
5	11.56
10	4.13
15	− 2.46
20	− 8.33

TABLE 8.4

NPV at different discount rates

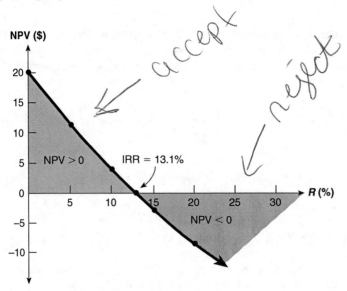

FIGURE 8.4

An NPV profile

y-axis, and the discount rates on the horizontal axis, or x-axis. If we had a very large number of points, the resulting picture would be a smooth curve called a **net present value profile**. Figure 8.4 illustrates the NPV profile for this project. Beginning with a 0 percent discount rate, we have $20 plotted directly on the y-axis. As the discount rate increases, the NPV declines smoothly. Where will the curve cut through the x-axis? This will occur where the NPV is just equal to zero, so it will happen right at the IRR of 13.1 percent.

In our example, the NPV rule and the IRR rule lead to identical accept-reject decisions. We will accept an investment using the IRR rule if the required return is less than 13.1 percent. As Figure 8.4 illustrates, however, the NPV is positive at any discount rate less than 13.1 percent, so we would accept the investment using the NPV rule as well. The two rules are equivalent in this case.

net present value profile

A graphical representation of the relationship between an investment's NPVs and various discount rates.

EXAMPLE 8.3   Calculating the IRR

A project has a total up-front cost of $435.44. The cash flows are $100 in the first year, $200 in the second year, and $300 in the third year. What's the IRR? If we require an 18 percent return, should we take this investment?

We'll describe the NPV profile and find the IRR by calculating some NPVs at different discount rates. You should check our answers for practice. Beginning with 0 percent, we have:

Discount Rate	NPV
0%	$164.56
5	100.36
10	46.15
15	.00
20	− 39.61

The NPV is zero at 15 percent, so 15 percent is the IRR. If we require an 18 percent return, then we should not take the investment. The reason is that the NPV is negative at 18 percent (verify that it is −$24.47). The IRR rule tells us the same thing in this case. We shouldn't take this investment because its 15 percent return is below our required 18 percent return.

At this point, you may be wondering whether the IRR and NPV rules always lead to identical decisions. The answer is yes as long as two very important conditions are met. First, the project's cash flows must be *conventional,* meaning that the first cash flow (the initial investment) is negative and all the rest are positive. Second, the project must be *independent,* meaning that the decision to accept or reject this project does not affect the decision to accept or reject any other. The first of these conditions is typically met, but the second often is not. In any case, when one or both of these conditions are not met, problems can arise. We discuss some of these in a moment.

Calculating IRRs with a Spreadsheet   SPREADSHEET STRATEGIES

Because IRRs are so tedious to calculate by hand, financial calculators and, especially, spreadsheets are generally used. The procedures used by various financial calculators are too different for us to illustrate here, so we will focus on using a spreadsheet (financial calculators are covered in Appendix D). As the following example illustrates, using a spreadsheet is very easy:

	A	B	C	D	E	F	G	H
1								
2			Using a spreadsheet to calculate internal rates of return					
3								
4	Suppose we have a four-year project that costs $500. The cash flows over the four-year life will be							
5	$100, $200, $300, and $400. What is the IRR?							
6								
7		Year	Cash flow					
8		0	−$500					
9		1	100		IRR =	27.3%		
10		2	200					
11		3	300					
12		4	400					
13								
14								
15	The formula entered in cell F9 is = IRR(C8:C12). Notice that the Year 0 cash flow has a negative sign,							
16	representing the initial cost of the project.							
17								

Problems with the IRR

The problems with the IRR come about when the cash flows are not conventional or when we are trying to compare two or more investments to see which is best. In the first case, surprisingly, the simple question "What's the return?" can become very difficult to answer. In the second case, the IRR can be a misleading guide.

Nonconventional Cash Flows   Suppose we have a strip-mining project that requires a $60 investment. Our cash flow in the first year will be $155. In the second year, the mine is depleted, but we have to spend $100 to restore the terrain. As Figure 8.5 illustrates, both the first and third cash flows are negative.

To find the IRR on this project, we can calculate the NPV at various rates:

Discount Rate	NPV
0%	−$5.00
10	− 1.74
20	− .28
30	.06
40	− .31

The NPV appears to be behaving in a very peculiar fashion here. First, as the discount rate increases from 0 percent to 30 percent, the NPV starts out negative and becomes positive. This seems backward because the NPV is rising as the discount rate rises. It then starts getting smaller and becomes negative again. What's the IRR? To find out, we draw the NPV profile in Figure 8.6.

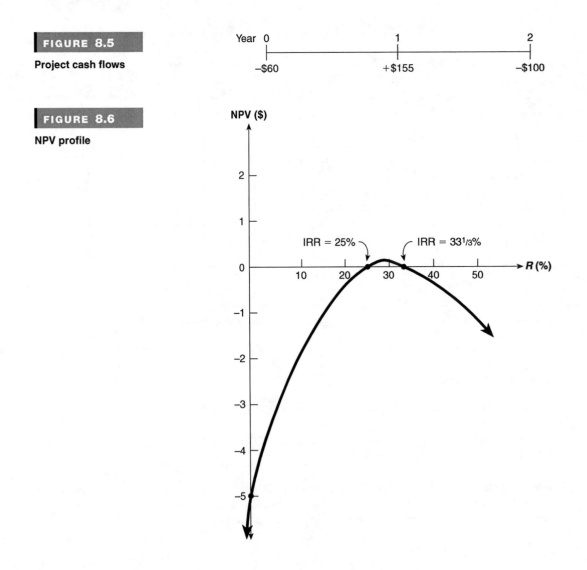

FIGURE 8.5

Project cash flows

FIGURE 8.6

NPV profile

In Figure 8.6, notice that the NPV is zero when the discount rate is 25 percent, so this is the IRR. Or is it? The NPV is also zero at 33⅓ percent. Which of these is correct? The answer is both or neither; more precisely, there is no unambiguously correct answer. This is the **multiple rates of return** problem. Many computer spreadsheet packages aren't aware of this problem and just report the first IRR that is found. Others report only the smallest positive IRR, even though this answer is no better than any other. For example, if you enter this problem in our spreadsheet above, it will simply report that the IRR is 25 percent.

In our current example, the IRR rule breaks down completely. Suppose our required return were 10 percent. Should we take this investment? Both IRRs are greater than 10 percent, so, by the IRR rule, maybe we should. However, as Figure 8.6 shows, the NPV is negative at any discount rate less than 25 percent, so this is not a good investment. When should we take it? Looking at Figure 8.6 one last time, we see that the NPV is positive only if our required return is between 25 percent and 33⅓ percent.

The moral of the story is that when the cash flows aren't conventional, strange things can start to happen to the IRR. This is not anything to get upset about, however, because the NPV rule, as always, works just fine. This illustrates that, oddly enough, the obvious question "What's the rate of return?" may not always have a good answer.

multiple rates of return

The possibility that more than one discount rate makes the NPV of an investment zero.

What's the IRR? EXAMPLE 8.4

You are looking at an investment that requires you to invest $51 today. You'll get $100 in one year, but you must pay out $50 in two years. What is the IRR on this investment?

You're on the alert now to the nonconventional cash flow problem, so you probably wouldn't be surprised to see more than one IRR. However, if you start looking for an IRR by trial and error, it will take you a long time. The reason is that there is no IRR. The NPV is negative at every discount rate, so we shouldn't take this investment under any circumstances. What's the return on this investment? Your guess is as good as ours.

Mutually Exclusive Investments   Even if there is a single IRR, another problem can arise concerning **mutually exclusive investment decisions**. If two investments, X and Y, are mutually exclusive, then taking one of them means that we cannot take the other. Two projects that are not mutually exclusive are said to be independent. For example, if we own one corner lot, then we can build a gas station or an apartment building, but not both. These are mutually exclusive alternatives.

Thus far, we have asked whether or not a given investment is worth undertaking. There is a related question, however, that comes up very often: Given two or more mutually exclusive investments, which one is the best? The answer is simple enough: The best one is the one with the largest NPV. Can we also say that the best one has the highest return? As we show, the answer is no.

To illustrate the problem with the IRR rule and mutually exclusive investments, consider the cash flows from the following two mutually exclusive investments:

mutually exclusive investment decisions

A situation where taking one investment prevents the taking of another.

Year	Investment A	Investment B
0	−$100	−$100
1	50	20
2	40	40
3	40	50
4	30	60

The IRR for A is 24 percent, and the IRR for B is 21 percent. Since these investments are mutually exclusive, we can only take one of them. Simple intuition suggests that Investment A is better because of its higher return. Unfortunately, simple intuition is not always correct.

To see why Investment A is not necessarily the better of the two investments, we've calculated the NPV of these investments for different required returns:

Discount Rate	NPV (A)	NPV (B)
0%	$60.00	$70.00
5	43.13	47.88
10	29.06	29.79
15	17.18	14.82
20	7.06	2.31
25	− 1.63	− 8.22

The IRR for A (24 percent) is larger than the IRR for B (21 percent). However, if you compare the NPVs, you'll see that which investment has the higher NPV depends on our required return. B has greater total cash flow, but it pays back more slowly than A. As a result, it has a higher NPV at lower discount rates.

In our example, the NPV and IRR rankings conflict for some discount rates. If our required return is 10 percent, for instance, then B has the higher NPV and is thus the better of the two, even though A has the higher return. If our required return is 15 percent, then there is no ranking conflict: A is better.

The conflict between the IRR and NPV for mutually exclusive investments can be illustrated by plotting their NPV profiles as we have done in Figure 8.7. In Figure 8.7,

FIGURE 8.7

NPV profiles for mutually exclusive investments

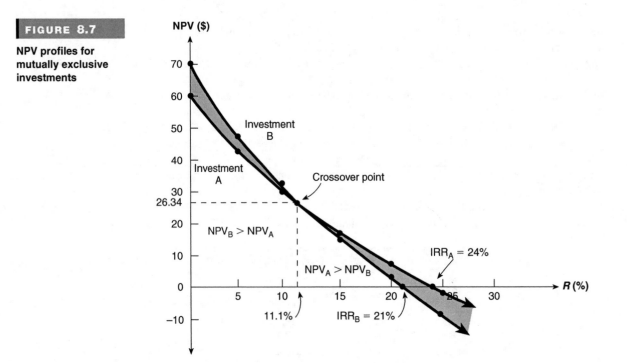

notice that the NPV profiles cross at 11.1 percent. Notice also that at any discount rate less than 11.1 percent, the NPV for B is higher. In this range, taking B benefits us more than taking A, even though A's IRR is higher. At any rate greater than 11.1 percent, Investment A has the greater NPV.

This example illustrates that whenever we have mutually exclusive projects, we shouldn't rank them based on their returns. More generally, anytime we are comparing investments to determine which is best, IRRs can be misleading. Instead, we need to look at the relative NPVs to avoid the possibility of choosing incorrectly. Remember, we're ultimately interested in creating value for the shareholders, so the option with the higher NPV is preferred, regardless of the relative returns.

If this seems counterintuitive, think of it this way. Suppose you have two investments. One has a 10 percent return and makes you $100 richer immediately. The other has a 20 percent return and makes you $50 richer immediately. Which one do you like better? We would rather have $100 than $50, regardless of the returns, so we like the first one better.

As we saw from Figure 8.7, the crossover rate for Investment A and Investment B is 11.1 percent. You might be wondering how we got this number. Actually, the calculation is fairly easy. We begin by subtracting the cash flows from one project from the cash flows of the second project. In this case, we will subtract Investment B from Investment A. Doing so, we get:

Year	Investment A	Investment B	Cash Flow Difference (A − B)
0	−$100	−$100	$ 0
1	50	20	30
2	40	40	0
3	40	50	−10
4	30	60	−30

Now all we have to do is calculate the IRR for these differential cash flows, which works out to be 11.1 percent. Verify for yourself that if you subtract Investment A's cash flows from Investment B's cash flows the crossover rate is still 11.1 percent, so it doesn't matter which one you subtract from which.

Redeeming Qualities of the IRR

Despite its flaws, the IRR is very popular in practice, more so than even the NPV. It probably survives because it fills a need that the NPV does not. In analyzing investments, people in general, and financial analysts in particular, seem to prefer talking about rates of return rather than dollar values.

In a similar vein, the IRR also appears to provide a simple way of communicating information about a proposal. One manager might say to another, "Remodeling the clerical wing has a 20 percent return." This may somehow be simpler than saying, "At a 10 percent discount rate, the net present value is $4,000."

Finally, under certain circumstances, the IRR may have a practical advantage over the NPV. We can't estimate the NPV unless we know the appropriate discount rate, but we can still estimate the IRR. Suppose we didn't know the required return on an investment, but we found, for example, that it had a 40 percent return. We would probably be inclined to take it since it is very unlikely that the required return would be that high. The advantages and disadvantages of the IRR are summarized below.

Advantages and Disadvantages of the Internal Rate of Return	
Advantages	**Disadvantages**
1. Closely related to NPV, often leading to identical decisions.	1. May result in multiple answers with nonconventional cash flows.
2. Easy to understand and communicate.	2. May lead to incorrect decisions in comparisons of mutually exclusive investments.

CONCEPT QUESTIONS

8.4a   Under what circumstances will the IRR and NPV rules lead to the same accept-reject decisions? When might they conflict?

8.4b   Is it generally true that an advantage of the IRR rule over the NPV rule is that we don't need to know the required return to use the IRR rule?

8.5 | THE PROFITABILITY INDEX

profitability index (PI)

The present value of an investment's future cash flows divided by its initial cost. Also, benefit-cost ratio.

Another method used to evaluate projects involves the **profitability index (PI)**, or benefit-cost ratio. This index is defined as the present value of the future cash flows divided by the initial investment. So, if a project costs $200 and the present value of its future cash flows is $220, the profitability index value would be $220/200 = 1.10. Notice that the NPV for this investment is $20, so it is a desirable investment.

More generally, if a project has a positive NPV, then the present value of the future cash flows must be bigger than the initial investment. The profitability index would thus be bigger than 1.00 for a positive NPV investment and less than 1.00 for a negative NPV investment.

How do we interpret the profitability index? In our example, the PI was 1.10. This tells us that, per dollar invested, $1.10 in value or $.10 in NPV results. The profitability index thus measures "bang for the buck," that is, the value created per dollar invested. For this reason, it is often proposed as a measure of performance for government or other not-for-profit investments. Also, when capital is scarce, it may make sense to allocate it to those projects with the highest PIs.

The PI is obviously very similar to the NPV. However, consider an investment that costs $5 and has a $10 present value and an investment that costs $100 with a $150 present value. The first of these investments has an NPV of $5 and a PI of 2. The second has an NPV of $50 and a PI of 1.50. If these are mutually exclusive investments, then the second one is preferred, even though it has a lower PI. This ranking problem is very similar to the IRR ranking problem we saw in the previous section. In all, there seems to be little reason to rely on the PI instead of the NPV. Our discussion of the PI is summarized below.

Advantages and Disadvantages of the Profitability Index	
Advantages	**Disadvantages**
1. Closely related to NPV, generally leading to identical decisions.	1. May lead to incorrect decisions in comparisons of mutually exclusive investments.
2. Easy to understand and communicate.	
3. May be useful when available investment funds are limited.	

THE PRACTICE OF CAPITAL BUDGETING | 8.6

Given that NPV seems to be telling us directly what we want to know, you might be wondering why there are so many other procedures and why alternative procedures are commonly used. Recall that we are trying to make an investment decision and that we are frequently operating under considerable uncertainty about the future. We can only *estimate* the NPV of an investment in this case. The resulting estimate can be very "soft," meaning that the true NPV might be quite different.

Because the true NPV is unknown, the astute financial manager seeks clues to assess whether the estimated NPV is reliable. For this reason, firms would typically use multiple criteria for evaluating a proposal. For example, suppose we have an investment with a positive estimated NPV. Based on our experience with other projects, this one appears to have a short payback and a very high AAR. In this case, the different indicators seem to agree that it's "all systems go." Put another way, the payback and the AAR are consistent with the conclusion that the NPV is positive.

On the other hand, suppose we had a positive estimated NPV, a long payback, and a low AAR. This could still be a good investment, but it looks like we need to be much more careful in making the decision since we are getting conflicting signals. If the estimated NPV is based on projections in which we have little confidence, then further analysis is probably in order. We will consider how to go about this analysis in more detail in the next chapter.

There have been a number of surveys conducted asking firms what types of investment criteria they actually use. Table 8.5 summarizes the results of several of these. The first part of the table is a historical comparison looking at the primary capital budgeting techniques used by large firms through time. In 1959, only 19 percent of the firms surveyed used either IRR or NPV, and 68 percent used either payback periods or accounting returns. It is clear that, by the 1980s, IRR and NPV had become the dominant criteria.

Panel B of Table 8.5 summarizes the results of a 1999 survey of chief financial officers (CFOs) at both large and small firms in the United States. A total of 392 CFOs responded. What is shown is the percentage of CFOs who always or almost always use the various capital budgeting techniques we described in this chapter. Not surprisingly, IRR and NPV are the two most widely used techniques, particularly at larger firms. However, over half of the respondents always, or almost always, use the payback criterion as well. In fact, among smaller firms, payback is used just about as much as NPV and IRR. Less commonly used are accounting rates of return and the profitability index. For quick reference, these criteria are briefly summarized in Table 8.6.

TABLE 8.5   Capital budgeting techniques in practice

A. Historical Comparison of the Primary Use of Various Capital Budgeting Techniques							
	1959	1964	1970	1975	1977	1979	1981
Payback period	34%	24%	12%	15%	9%	10%	5.0%
Average accounting return (AAR)	34	30	26	10	25	14	10.7
Internal rate of return (IRR)	19	38	57	37	54	60	65.3
Net present value (NPV)	—	—	—	26	10	14	16.5
IRR or NPV	19	38	57	63	64	74	81.8

B. Percentage of CFOs Who Always or Almost Always Use a Given Technique in 1999				
Capital Budgeting Technique	Percentage Always or Almost Always Use	Average Score Scale is 4 (always) to 0 (never)		
		Overall	Large Firms	Small Firms
Internal rate of return	76%	3.09	3.41	2.87
Net present value	75	3.08	3.42	2.83
Payback period	57	2.53	2.25	2.72
Accounting rate of return	20	1.34	1.25	1.41
Profitability index	12	0.83	0.75	0.88

Sources: J. R. Graham and C. R. Harvey, "The Theory and Practice of Corporate Finance: Evidence from the Field," *Journal of Financial Economics,* May–June 2001, pp. 187–244; J. S. Moore and A. K. Reichert, "An Analysis of the Financial Management Techniques Currently Employed by Large U.S. Corporations," *Journal of Business Finance and Accounting,* Winter 1983, pp. 623–45; M. T. Stanley and S. R. Block, "A Survey of Multinational Capital Budgeting," *The Financial Review,* March 1984, pp. 36–51.

TABLE 8.6   Summary of investment criteria

I. Discounted cash flow criteria
   A. *Net present value (NPV).* The NPV of an investment is the difference between its market value and its cost. The NPV rule is to take a project if its NPV is positive. NPV is frequently estimated by calculating the present value of the future cash flows (to estimate market value) and then subtracting the cost. NPV has no serious flaws; it is the preferred decision criterion.
   B. *Internal rate of return (IRR).* The IRR is the discount rate that makes the estimated NPV of an investment equal to zero; it is sometimes called the *discounted cash flow (DCF) return.* The IRR rule is to take a project when its IRR exceeds the required return. IRR is closely related to NPV, and it leads to exactly the same decisions as NPV for conventional, independent projects. When project cash flows are not conventional, there may be no IRR or there may be more than one. More seriously, the IRR cannot be used to rank mutually exclusive projects; the project with the highest IRR is not necessarily the preferred investment.
   C. *Profitability index (PI).* The PI, also called the *benefit-cost ratio,* is the ratio of present value to cost. The PI rule is to take an investment if the index exceeds 1. The PI measures the present value of an investment per dollar invested. It is quite similar to NPV, but, like IRR, it cannot be used to rank mutually exclusive projects. However, it is sometimes used to rank projects when a firm has more positive NPV investments than it can currently finance.

II. Payback criteria
   A. *Payback period.* The payback period is the length of time until the sum of an investment's cash flows equals its cost. The payback period rule is to take a project if its payback is *less* than some cutoff. The payback period is a flawed criterion primarily because it ignores risk, the time value of money, and cash flows beyond the cutoff point.

III. Accounting criteria
   A. *Average accounting return (AAR).* The AAR is a measure of accounting profit relative to book value. It is *not* related to the IRR, but it is similar to the accounting return on assets (ROA) measure in Chapter 3. The AAR rule is to take an investment if its AAR exceeds a benchmark AAR. The AAR is seriously flawed for a variety of reasons, and it has little to recommend it.

SUMMARY AND CONCLUSIONS

This chapter has covered the different criteria used to evaluate proposed investments. The five criteria, in the order in which we discussed them, are:

1. Net present value (NPV)
2. Payback period
3. Average accounting return (AAR)
4. Internal rate of return (IRR)
5. Profitability index (PI)

We illustrated how to calculate each of these and discussed the interpretation of the results. We also described the advantages and disadvantages of each of them. Ultimately, a good capital budgeting criterion must tell us two things. First, is a particular project a good investment? Second, if we have more than one good project, but we can only take one of them, which one should we take? The main point of this chapter is that only the NPV criterion can always provide the correct answer to both questions.

For this reason, NPV is one of the two or three most important concepts in finance, and we will refer to it many times in the chapters ahead. When we do, keep two things in mind: (1) NPV is always just the difference between the market value of an asset or project and its cost and (2) the financial manager acts in the shareholders' best interests by identifying and taking positive NPV projects.

Finally, we noted that NPVs can't normally be observed in the market; instead, they must be estimated. Because there is always the possibility of a poor estimate, financial managers use multiple criteria for examining projects. These other criteria provide additional information about whether a project truly has a positive NPV.

CHAPTER REVIEW AND SELF-TEST PROBLEMS

8.1 Investment Criteria.   This problem will give you some practice calculating NPVs and paybacks. A proposed overseas expansion has the following cash flows:

Year	Cash Flow
0	−$100
1	50
2	40
3	40
4	15

Calculate the payback and NPV at a required return of 15 percent.

8.2 Mutually Exclusive Investments.   Consider the following two mutually exclusive investments. Calculate the IRR for each. Under what circumstances will the IRR and NPV criteria rank the two projects differently?

Year	Investment A	Investment B
0	−$100	−$100
1	50	70
2	70	75
3	40	10

8.3   Average Accounting Return.   You are looking at a three-year project with a projected net income of $1,000 in Year 1, $2,000 in Year 2, and $4,000 in Year 3. The cost is $9,000, which will be depreciated straight-line to zero over the three-year life of the project. What is the average accounting return, or AAR?

◼ Answers to Chapter Review and Self-Test Problems

8.1   In the table below, we have listed the cash flows and their discounted values (at 15 percent).

	Cash Flow	
Year	Undiscounted	Discounted (at 15%)
1	$ 50	$ 43.48
2	40	30.25
3	40	26.30
4	15	8.58
Total	$145	$108.6

Recall that the initial investment is $100. Examining the undiscounted cash flows, we see that the payback occurs between Years 2 and 3. The cash flows for the first two years are $90 total, so, going into the third year, we are short by $10. The total cash flow in Year 3 is $40, so the payback is 2 + $10/40 = 2.25 years.

Looking at the discounted cash flows, we see that the sum is $108.6, so the NPV is $8.6.

8.2   To calculate the IRR, we might try some guesses as in the following table:

Discount Rate	NPV(A)	NPV(B)
0%	$60.00	$55.00
10	33.36	33.13
20	13.43	16.20
30	− 1.91	2.78
40	−13.99	− 8.09

Several things are immediately apparent from our guesses. First, the IRR on A must be just a little less than 30 percent (why?). With some more effort, we find that it's 28.61 percent. For B, the IRR must be a little more than 30 percent (again, why?); it works out to be 32.37 percent. Also, notice that at 10 percent, the NPVs are very close, indicating that the NPV profiles cross in that vicinity. Verify that the NPVs are the same at 10.61 percent.

Now, the IRR for B is always higher. As we've seen, A has the larger NPV for any discount rate less than 10.61 percent, so the NPV and IRR rankings will conflict in that range. Remember, if there's a conflict, we will go with the higher NPV. Our decision rule is thus very simple: Take A if the required return is less than 10.61 percent, take B if the required return is between 10.61 percent and 32.37 percent (the IRR on B), and take neither if the required return is more than 32.37 percent.

8.3   Here we need to calculate the ratio of average net income to average book value to get the AAR. Average net income is:

Average net income = ($1,000 + 2,000 + 4,000)/3
= $2,333.33

Average book value is:

Average book value = $9,000/2 = $4,500

So the average accounting return is:

AAR = $2,333.33/4,500 = 51.85%

This is an impressive return. Remember, however, that it isn't really a rate of return like an interest rate or an IRR, so the size doesn't tell us a lot. In particular, our money is probably not going to grow at 51.85 percent per year, sorry to say.

CRITICAL THINKING AND CONCEPTS REVIEW

8.1   Payback Period and Net Present Value.   If a project with conventional cash flows has a payback period less than its life, can you definitively state the algebraic sign of the NPV? Why or why not?

8.2   Net Present Value.   Suppose a project has conventional cash flows and a positive NPV. What do you know about its payback? Its profitability index? Its IRR? Explain.

8.3   Payback Period.   Concerning payback:

a.   Describe how the payback period is calculated and describe the information this measure provides about a sequence of cash flows. What is the payback criterion decision rule?

b.   What are the problems associated with using the payback period as a means of evaluating cash flows?

c.   What are the advantages of using the payback period to evaluate cash flows? Are there any circumstances under which using payback might be appropriate? Explain.

8.4   Average Accounting Return.   Concerning AAR:

a.   Describe how the average accounting return is usually calculated and describe the information this measure provides about a sequence of cash flows. What is the AAR criterion decision rule?

b.   What are the problems associated with using the AAR as a means of evaluating a project's cash flows? What underlying feature of AAR is most troubling to you from a financial perspective? Does the AAR have any redeeming qualities?

8.5   Net Present Value.   Concerning NPV:

a.   Describe how NPV is calculated and describe the information this measure provides about a sequence of cash flows. What is the NPV criterion decision rule?

b.   Why is NPV considered to be a superior method of evaluating the cash flows from a project? Suppose the NPV for a project's cash flows is computed to be $2,500. What does this number represent with respect to the firm's shareholders?

8.6 **Internal Rate of Return.**   Concerning IRR:

    a. Describe how the IRR is calculated, and describe the information this measure provides about a sequence of cash flows. What is the IRR criterion decision rule?

    b. What is the relationship between IRR and NPV? Are there any situations in which you might prefer one method over the other? Explain.

    c. Despite its shortcomings in some situations, why do most financial managers use IRR along with NPV when evaluating projects? Can you think of a situation in which IRR might be a more appropriate measure to use than NPV? Explain.

8.7 **Profitability Index.**   Concerning the profitability index:

    a. Describe how the profitability index is calculated and describe the information this measure provides about a sequence of cash flows. What is the profitability index decision rule?

    b. What is the relationship between the profitability index and the NPV? Are there any situations in which you might prefer one method over the other? Explain.

8.8 **Payback and Internal Rate of Return.**   A project has perpetual cash flows of C per period, a cost of I, and a required return of R. What is the relationship between the project's payback and its IRR? What implications does your answer have for long-lived projects with relatively constant cash flows?

8.9 **International Investment Projects.**   In November 2004 automobile manufacturer Honda announced plans to build an automatic transmission plant in Georgia and expand its transmission plant in Ohio. Honda apparently felt that it would be better able to compete and create value with U.S.-based facilities. Other companies such as Fuji Film and Swiss chemical company Lonza have reached similar conclusions and taken similar actions. What are some of the reasons that foreign manufacturers of products as diverse as automobiles, film, and chemicals might arrive at this same conclusion?

8.10 **Capital Budgeting Problems.**   What are some of the difficulties that might come up in actual applications of the various criteria we discussed in this chapter? Which one would be the easiest to implement in actual applications? The most difficult?

8.11 **Capital Budgeting in Not-for-Profit Entities.**   Are the capital budgeting criteria we discussed applicable to not-for-profit corporations? How should such entities make capital budgeting decisions? What about the U.S. government? Should it evaluate spending proposals using these techniques?

8.12 **Internal Rate of Return.**   In a previous chapter, we discussed the yield to maturity (YTM) of a bond. In what ways are the IRR and the YTM similar? How are they different?

QUESTIONS AND PROBLEMS

Basic
(Questions 1–21)

    1. Calculating Payback.   What is the payback period for the following set of cash flows?

Year	Cash Flow
0	−$2,500
1	600
2	1,300
3	800
4	600

2. **Calculating Payback.**   An investment project provides cash inflows of $830 per year for eight years. What is the project payback period if the initial cost is $3,400? What if the initial cost is $4,450? What if it is $6,800?

3. **Calculating Payback.**   Offshore Drilling Products, Inc., imposes a payback cutoff of three years for its international investment projects. If the company has the following two projects available, should it accept either of them?

Year	Cash Flow (A)	Cash Flow (B)
0	−$45,000	−$ 90,000
1	17,000	20,000
2	20,000	25,000
3	18,000	30,000
4	9,000	250,000

4. **Calculating AAR.**   You're trying to determine whether or not to expand your business by building a new manufacturing plant. The plant has an installation cost of $14 million, which will be depreciated straight-line to zero over its four-year life. If the plant has projected net income of $1,315,000, $1,846,000, $1,523,000, and $1,308,000 over these four years, what is the project's average accounting return (AAR)?

5. **Calculating IRR.**   A firm evaluates all of its projects by applying the IRR rule. If the required return is 18 percent, should the firm accept the following project?

Year	Cash Flow
0	−$100,000
1	45,000
2	52,000
3	43,000

6. **Calculating NPV.**   For the cash flows in the previous problem, suppose the firm uses the NPV decision rule. At a required return of 11 percent, should the firm accept this project? What if the required return was 23 percent?

7. **Calculating NPV and IRR.**   A project that provides annual cash flows of $1,200 for nine years costs $5,200 today. Is this a good project if the required return is 8 percent? What if it's 24 percent? At what discount rate would you be indifferent between accepting the project and rejecting it?

8. **Calculating IRR.**   What is the IRR of the following set of cash flows?

Year	Cash Flow
0	−$28,000
1	12,500
2	18,700
3	11,800

9. Calculating NPV. For the cash flows in the previous problem, what is the NPV at a discount rate of zero percent? What if the discount rate is 10 percent? If it is 20 percent? If it is 30 percent?

10. NPV versus IRR. Bates & Reid, LLC, has identified the following two mutually exclusive projects:

Year	Cash Flow (A)	Cash Flow (B)
0	−$30,000	−$30,000
1	16,000	6,000
2	13,000	11,000
3	8,000	12,000
4	5,000	19,000

    a. What is the IRR for each of these projects? If you apply the IRR decision rule, which project should the company accept? Is this decision necessarily correct?

    b. If the required return is 11 percent, what is the NPV for each of these projects? Which project will you choose if you apply the NPV decision rule?

    c. Over what range of discount rates would you choose Project A? Project B? At what discount rate would you be indifferent between these two projects? Explain.

11. NPV versus IRR. Consider the following two mutually exclusive projects:

Year	Cash Flow (X)	Cash Flow (Y)
0	−$5,000	−$5,000
1	2,700	2,300
2	1,700	1,800
3	2,300	2,700

Sketch the NPV profiles for X and Y over a range of discount rates from zero to 25 percent. What is the crossover rate for these two projects?

12. Problems with IRR. Brazz Petroleum, Inc., is trying to evaluate a generation project with the following cash flows:

Year	Cash Flow
0	−$28,000,000
1	53,000,000
2	− 8,000,000

a. If the company requires a 10 percent return on its investments, should it accept this project? Why?

b. Compute the IRR for this project. How many IRRs are there? If you apply the IRR decision rule, should you accept the project or not? What's going on here?

13. Calculating Profitability Index. What is the profitability index for the following set of cash flows if the relevant discount rate is 10 percent? What if the discount rate is 15 percent? If it is 22 percent?

Year	Cash Flow
0	−$15,000
1	9,000
2	6,000
3	4,500

14. Problems with Profitability Index. The Becca Corporation is trying to choose between the following two mutually exclusive design projects:

Year	Cash Flow (I)	Cash Flow (II)
0	−$35,000	−$5,500
1	12,000	2,800
2	16,000	2,600
3	19,000	2,400

a. If the required return is 11 percent and Becca applies the profitability index decision rule, which project should the firm accept?

b. If the company applies the NPV decision rule, which project should it take?

c. Explain why your answers in (*a*) and (*b*) are different.

15. Comparing Investment Criteria. Consider the following two mutually exclusive projects:

Year	Cash Flow (A)	Cash Flow (B)
0	−$252,000	−$24,000
1	18,000	14,400
2	36,000	12,600
3	38,400	11,400
4	510,000	9,800

Whichever project you choose, if any, you require a 15 percent return on your investment.

a. If you apply the payback criterion, which investment will you choose? Why?

b. If you apply the NPV criterion, which investment will you choose? Why?

c. If you apply the IRR criterion, which investment will you choose? Why?

d. If you apply the profitability index criterion, which investment will you choose? Why?

e. Based on your answers in (*a*) through (*d*), which project will you finally choose? Why?

16. **NPV and IRR.**   Boston Company is presented with the following two mutually exclusive projects. The required return for both projects is 15 percent.

Year	Project M	Project N
0	−$175,000	−$280,000
1	65,000	100,000
2	85,000	140,000
3	75,000	120,000
4	65,000	80,000

    a.   What is the IRR for each project?

    b.   What is the NPV for each project?

    c.   Which, if either, of the projects should the company accept?

17. **NPV and Profitability Index.**   Humboldt Manufacturing has the following two possible projects. The required return is 12 percent.

Year	Project Y	Project Z
0	−$45,000	−$65,000
1	18,000	26,000
2	17,000	24,000
3	16,000	22,000
4	15,000	22,000

    a.   What is the profitability index for each project?

    b.   What is the NPV for each project?

    c.   Which, if either, of the projects should the company accept?

18. **Crossover Point.**   Cutler Enterprises has gathered projected cash flows for two projects. At what interest rate would Cutler be indifferent between the two projects? Which project is better if the required return is above this interest rate? Why?

Year	Project I	Project J
0	−$120,000	−$120,000
1	50,000	43,000
2	48,000	46,000
3	46,000	49,000
4	44,000	52,000

19. **Payback Period and IRR.**   Suppose you have a project with a payback period exactly equal to the life of the project. What do you know about the IRR of the project? Suppose that the payback period is never. What do you know about the IRR of the project now?

20. **NPV and Discount Rates.**   An investment has an installed cost of $513,250. The cash flows over the four-year life of the investment are projected to be $180,124, $195,467, $141,386, and $130,287. If the discount rate is zero, what is the NPV? If the discount rate is infinite, what is the NPV? At what discount rate is the NPV just equal to zero? Sketch the NPV profile for this investment based on these three points.

21. NPV and Payback Period.   Kaleb Konstruction, Inc., has the following mutually exclusive projects available. The company has historically used a three-year cutoff for projects. The required return is 10 percent.

Year	Project F	Project G
0	−$150,000	−$240,000
1	80,000	60,000
2	60,000	70,000
3	75,000	90,000
4	60,000	140,000
5	50,000	120,000

   a.   Calculate the payback period for both projects.
   b.   Calculate the NPV for both projects.
   c.   Which project, if any, should the company accept?

22. Crossover and NPV.   Burns Auto has the following two mutually exclusive projects available.

Intermediate
(Questions 22–26)

Year	Project R	Project S
0	−$40,000	−$58,000
1	20,000	24,000
2	15,000	24,000
3	15,000	18,000
4	8,000	12,000
5	8,000	12,000

What is the crossover rate for these two projects? What is the NPV of each project at the crossover rate?

23. Calculating IRR.   A project has the following cash flows:

Year	Cash Flow
0	$64,000
1	− 30,000
2	− 48,000

What is the IRR for this project? If the required return is 12 percent, should the firm accept the project? What is the NPV of this project? What is the NPV of the project if the required return is 0 percent? 24 percent? What is going on here? Sketch the NPV profile to help you with your answer.

24. Multiple IRRs.   This problem is useful for testing the ability of financial calculators and computer software. Consider the following cash flows. When should we take this project? (Hint: search for IRRs between 20 percent and 70 percent.)

Year	Cash Flow
0	−$ 504
1	2,862
2	− 6,070
3	5,700
4	− 2,000

25. **NPV and the Profitability Index.**   If we define the NPV index as the ratio of NPV to cost, what is the relationship between this index and the profitability index?

26. **Cash Flow Intuition.**   A project has an initial cost of I, has a required return of R, and pays C annually for N years.

   a.   Find C in terms of I and N such that the project has a payback period just equal to its life.

   b.   Find C in terms of I, N, and R such that this is a profitable project according to the NPV decision rule.

   c.   Find C in terms of I, N, and R such that the project has a benefit-cost ratio of 2.

WHAT'S ON THE WEB?

8.1   **Net Present Value.**   You have a project that has an initial cash outflow of $-\$20,000$ and cash inflows of $6,000, $5,000, $4,000, and $3,000, respectively, for the next four years. Go to www.datadynamica.com and follow the "On-line IRR NPV Calculator" link. Enter the cash flows. If the required return is 12 percent, what is the IRR of the project? The NPV?

8.2   **Internal Rate of Return.**   Using the online calculator from the previous problem, find the IRR for a project with cash flows of $-\$500$, $1,200, and $-\$400$. What is going on here?

www.mhhe.com/rwj

STUDENT PROBLEM MANUAL

for use with

ESSENTIALS OF CORPORATE FINANCE
Fifth Edition

CHAPTER 4

INTRODUCTION TO VALUATION:

THE TIME VALUE OF MONEY

CONCEPTS FOR REVIEW

Finance is sometimes called the "science of valuation" because virtually every decision faced by the financial manager ultimately comes down to how firm value will be affected. The core of the valuation process is the *time-value* model, which describes how cash flows to be paid or received at various points in time are valued. After reading this chapter, you will understand two concepts crucial to any valuation problem you will ever face: *present value* and *future value*.

CHAPTER HIGHLIGHTS

In this chapter and the next we discuss several basic financial calculations. When you understand the concepts in these chapters, you will be able to solve many of the 'mysteries' of everyday financial life. Therefore, in addition to providing the foundation for financial decision-making for corporate managers, the material in these chapters also has important applications for every consumer who makes a bank deposit or an investment, buys life insurance, or takes out an automobile or mortgage loan.

*Learning Tip: A thorough knowledge of this chapter is **essential** to an understanding of the material that follows. <u>This is one of the most important topics you will cover in this course.</u> And, since the topics in the chapter are developed sequentially, it is crucial that each is well understood before moving to the next.*

I. FUTURE VALUE AND COMPOUNDING (p. 3)

Investing for a Single Period (p. 3) A *future value* is the amount to which an initial dollar deposit (the *principal*) will grow when interest is compounded at a specified interest rate for a specified number of years. In general, the future value (FV) of an investment over a one-year period can be determined using the following equation:

$$FV = P \times (1 + r),$$ where P is the original principal and r is the annual interest rate.

Investing for More Than One Period (p. 3) If the principal is left on deposit for, say, two years, the future value depends on whether or not the interest earned during the first year is left on deposit during the second year. If not, then the deposit earns *simple interest* on original principal each year; that is, the interest received each year does not earn interest during any subsequent year. If the first year's interest *is* left on deposit to earn interest, then the interest earned in the second year will include interest on both the original principal and on the first year's interest. Since the depositor earns interest on the previous year's interest, this is referred to as *compound interest*, or the process of *compounding interest*.

The future value (FV) of the principal P invested for t years at an interest rate r is given by:

$$FV_t = P \times (1 + r)^t$$

The expression $(1 + r)^t$ is called the *future value interest factor*, or simply *future value factor*, and is sometimes abbreviated as FVIF(r,t). Future value interest factors appear in the text appendix.

II. PRESENT VALUE AND DISCOUNTING (p. 10)

The Single Period Case (p. 10) In this section we ask the following question: What deposit P is required today, in an account paying r% interest per annum, in order to have $X t years from now? P is the *present value* (henceforth *PV*) of $X to be received t years from now, when the appropriate interest rate is r%.

The process of computing a present value is *discounting*, and the interest rate used in a present value calculation is the *discount rate*. The present value of a single cash flow can be found as follows:

$$PV = FV/(1+r).$$

Present Values for Multiple Periods (p. 11) Further, the present value of dollars to be paid or received in t periods is equal to

$$PV = FV/(1+r)^t.$$

The term $1/(1 + r)^t$ in the above formula is the *present value interest factor* and is abbreviated PVIF(r,t). Since the process of calculating a present value is sometimes called discounting, we also refer to the term $1/(1 + r)^t$ as the *discount factor*. The process of computing a present value is referred to as *discounted cash flow (DCF)* valuation.

III. MORE ON PRESENT AND FUTURE VALUES (p. 14)

In this section, we discuss further the relationship between present values and future values; we also analyze some additional aspects of these concepts.

Present versus Future Value (p. 14) The basic equations developed above are, in fact, two algebraically equivalent versions of the same equation. That is, given the future value equation

$$FV_t = PV \times FVIF(r, t),$$

the corresponding present value equation is

$$PV = FV_t/FVIF(r, t) = FV_t \times 1/FVIF(r, t) = FV_t \times PVIF(r, t).$$

Determining the Discount Rate (p. 14) The basic present value equation contains four variables: present value (PV), future value at time t (FV$_t$), discount rate (r), and time (t). Given any three of these variables, we can always solve for the fourth.

Example: A recent *Barron's* article cited the example of a portfolio manager whose investments had increased in value from $64,000 in 1969 to $695,531 in 2000. What was the average annually compounded rate of return on his investment portfolio?

$$PV = FV/(1 + r)^t$$
$$\$64,000 = \$695,531/(1 + r)^{31}$$
$$\$695,531/\$64,000 = 10.86767 = (1 + r)^{31}$$
$$r = .08 = 8\%.$$

Finding the Number of Periods (p. 18) Similarly, we can solve for t, given PV, FV, and r. Refer to the previous example. Given an 8% annually compounded rate of return, how long would it take for $64,000 to grow to $695,531? Obviously, the answer is 31, found as follows:

Answer:

$$FV = PV \times (1 + r)^t$$
$$\$695,531 = \$64,000 \times (1.08)^t$$
$$t = 31$$

KEY TERMS AND CONCEPTS

Compounding - the process of accumulating interest over time to earn more interest. (p. 4)
Compound interest - interest earned on the principal and interest from prior periods. (p. 4)
Discount - to calculate the present value of some future amount. (p. 10)
Discounted cash flow (DCF) valuation - valuation calculating the present value of a future cash flow to determine its value today. (p. 11)
Discount rate - the rate used to calculate the present value of future cash flows. (p. 11)
Future value - the value of an investment after one or more periods. (Also *compound value*.) (p. 3)
Interest on interest - interest earned on the reinvestment of previous interest payments. (p. 4)
Present value - current value of future cash flows discounted at the appropriate discount rate. (p. 10)
Simple interest - interest earned only on the original principal amount invested. (p. 4)

CONCEPT TEST

1. When a deposit or investment earns interest on interest previously received, it is said to be earning _____; this process is referred to as _____. A _____ is the amount to which an initial deposit, called the _____, will grow when interest is compounded at a specified interest rate for a specified number of years. The future value (FV_t) of an initial deposit (PV) which earns interest at the rate r for t years is given by the following formula: $FV_t =$ _____ . The expression _____ is referred to as the *future value interest factor*, and is abbreviated as _____. (p. 3)

2. _____ is the process of accumulating interest over time to earn more interest. _____ is the interest earned on the principal and interest from prior periods. _____ interest, on the other hand, refers to interest earned only on the original principal invested. (p. 4)

3. A *present value* is the amount that must be invested today, at a specified _____, to grow to a specified _____, at a specified _____. The PV is dependent on three values: the _____, the amount of the _____, and the _____. Computing a PV is called _____. The rate used in the calculation is the _____. (p. 10)

4.   A PV can be calculated by substituting known values of the _____, the _____, and the _____ into the basic PV equation as follows: PV = _____ . Alternatively, we can rearrange the basic PV equation so that the PV is determined by multiplying the future value (FV) times the _____ of the FV interest factor: PV = _____ . The term _____ is called the present value interest factor (PVIF) and is abbreviated _____ . The PVIF can be determined from tables. The PVIF is also called the _____ and computing a PV is also referred to as _____ valuation. (p. 11)

5.   The *basic present value equation* states the relationship between present and future values. Specifically, it states that:

$$\text{_____} \times \text{_____} = FV_t, \text{ or } PV = \text{_____} = FV_t \times \text{_____} . \text{(p.14)}$$

ANSWERS TO CONCEPT TEST

1.   compound interest; compounding; future value; principal; $[PVH(1+r)^t]$; $[(1+r)^t]$; $FVIF(r,t)$
2.   Compounding; Compound interest; Simple
3.   interest rate; amount; future date; interest rate; future payment; time; discounting; discount rate
4.   interest rate; future payment; time period; $[FV_t/(1+r)^t]$; reciprocal; $FV_tH[1/(1+r)^t]$; $[1/(1+r)^t]$; $PVIF(r,t)$; discount factor; discounted cash flow
5. PV; $(1 + r)^t$; $FV_t/(1 + r)^t$; $[1/(1 + r)^t]$

PROBLEMS

1. If you deposit $10,000 today in a bank account paying 10.38%, how much will you have in one year? If you need $12,000 in one year, how much do you have to deposit today?

2. An art collector has the opportunity to invest in paintings; the investment requires an initial outlay of $2 million today. The collector is certain that he will be able to sell the paintings for $2.18 million one year from now. He also has the opportunity to invest in bank certificates of deposit which pay 10% per year. What is the future value of the $2 million if the collector elects to purchase a bank certificate of deposit? Is the investment in the paintings a good investment?

3. In Problem 2, what is the rate of return for the investment in paintings?

4. For the paintings described in Problem 2, what is the PV of the future cash flow the collector would receive if he sold the paintings one year from now? What is the value of the paintings to the collector?

5. Calculate the present value for each of the following cash flows to be received one year hence:

Future cash flow	Interest rate	Present value
$ 10,000	10%	
153,200	13%	
153,200	10%	
2,567,450	5%	
120,600	9%	

6. As a newly-minted MBA embarking on a career in investment banking, you naturally must own a black Jaguar XK8 immediately. The car costs $80,000. You also have to spend $3,248 on a blue pin-stripe suit. Your spendable income this year is $92,000, and next year it will be $96,000. Your routine living expenses this year will be $84,000. You plan to make up the difference between current income and current consumption by borrowing; the interest rate for the loan is 14% (ouch!) and you intend to repay the loan, plus interest, in one year. How much will you have left to spend next year?

7. An individual has the opportunity to invest $1000 today to acquire an asset which will generate $300 in income one year from today and which can be sold for $900 at that time. Determine the minimum level of the market interest rate for which this investment would be attractive.

8. An investment requires an initial outlay of $195. The cash inflow from this investment will be $114 one year from today (year 1) and $144 two years from today (year 2). The market rate of interest is 20%. Find the present value for this investment. Is the investment acceptable?

9. An entrepreneur purchased an asset for $200,000 that will produce a cash inflow of $300,000 one year from now. He plans to issue 100 shares of common stock to himself and sell 900 shares of stock to the general public. His business, which consists entirely of this one asset, will cease to exist after one year. The market rate of interest is 20%, and the future cash inflow to the firm is guaranteed. At what price per share should the entrepreneur sell the common stock? What gain will he realize?

10. What is the present value of $145 to be received in 5 years if the market interest rate is 8%?

CHAPTER 5

DISCOUNTED CASH FLOW VALUATION

CONCEPTS FOR REVIEW

As noted in the previous chapter, Finance is sometimes called the "science of valuation" because most of the decisions faced by financial managers boil down to how firm value will be affected. We considered the valuation of single cash flows to be paid or received at different points in time. Here we take the next logical step - we learn to value *streams of cash flows*.

CHAPTER HIGHLIGHTS

Before you get deeply into this chapter, be sure that you understand the concepts described in the previous one. Additionally, keep in mind that most of the valuation problems faced by professional financial managers (as well as by individual consumers) involve streams of cash flows, rather than single cash flows, making the concepts below even more important.

Learning Tip: We feel strongly enough about it that we reiterate a point made in the previous chapter: A thorough knowledge of Time Value principles is __essential__ to an understanding of Finance.

I. FUTURE AND PRESENT VALUES OF MULTIPLE CASH FLOWS (p. 28)

Future Value with Multiple Cash Flows (p. 28) In this section we describe how to compute the balance in an account when deposits are made over a period of years. One way is to compute the ending balance at the end of the first year using the appropriate FVIF(r, t), add the second deposit, compute the balance at the end of the second year, and continue to do so as long as necessary. Alternatively, we can use the compounding formula to obtain the future value of each deposit at year t and sum these future values. The result will be the same as that obtained using the first approach.

Present Value with Multiple Cash Flows (p. 31) Similarly, there are two ways to determine the present value of multiple cash flows: we can discount future payments year-by-year, or we can compute the present value of each future cash flow and then sum the separate present values to determine the total present value for all the flows. The two approaches are mathematically equivalent.

A Note on Cash Flow Timing (p. 35) Whether we are computing future values or present values, we must specify exactly *when* cash flows occur; we generally assume that cash flows occur at the *end* of a time period. More on this later.

II. VALUING LEVEL CASH FLOWS: ANNUITIES AND PERPETUITIES (p. 36)

An *annuity* is a series of equal cash flows that occur at regular intervals for a fixed number of time periods. If the payments occur at the __end__ of each time period, the annuity is an *ordinary annuity* or a *regular annuity*. If payments are at the __beginning__ of each time period, we call the annuity a *deferred annuity* or *annuity due*. A *perpetuity* is a perpetual annuity; that is, cash flows go on forever.

Present Value for Annuity Cash Flows (p. 37) When the series of cash flows is an ordinary annuity we can simplify the computation by finding the sum of the individual present value factors and multiplying by the cash flow amount (C). We denote the sum of the present value factors as PVIFA(r,t), which stands for present value interest factor for an annuity, and the present value (PV) equals

$$PV = C \times PVIFA(r, t)$$

where C represents the constant annuity payment. Values of PVIFA(r, t) can be found in the Appendix to the textbook. Alternatively, one can compute PVIFA(r,t) by using the following formula:

$$PVIFA(r, t) = (1 - [1/(1 + r)^t])/r = (1 - [PVIF(r, t)])/r.$$

Future Value for Annuities (p. 42) We can employ a similar approach to find the future value of an annuity. From Table A.4 we obtain the *future value interest factor for an annuity:* FVIFA(r, t). This factor, which is the sum of the individual future value interest factors for each payment in an annuity, is then multiplied by the payment amount, C, to determine the future value. Or FVIFA(r, t) can be computed from a formula, indicated below, and is then multiplied by the constant payment to calculate the future value of the annuity. The FVIFA(r, t) formula is:

$$FVIFA(r, t) = ((1 + r)^t - 1)/r = (FVIF(r, t) - 1)/r.$$

And the future value of an annuity, FV, equals $C \times FVIFA(r, t)$.

A Note on Annuities Due (p. 43) Previously it was pointed out that we generally assume that cash flows occur at the end of each period. However, there are instances in which cash flows occur at the *beginning* of each period (for example, an apartment lease). We define an *annuity due* as an annuity for which the cash flows occur at the beginning of each period. To value an annuity due, make the following adjustment to the ordinary annuity formula:

$$\text{Annuity due value} = \text{Ordinary annuity value} \times (1 + r).$$

Perpetuities (p. 43) A perpetuity (or perpetual annuity) is a series of equal cash flows, occurring at regular intervals, that continues <u>forever</u>. The present value of a perpetuity is

$$PV = C \times (1/r) = C/r.$$

III. COMPARING RATES: THE EFFECT OF COMPOUNDING PERIODS (p. 45)

So far, our discussion of future values and present values has assumed that interest rates are compounded annually. However, this isn't always the case.

Effective Annual Rates and Compounding (p. 45) Consider a bank that pays 12% interest per year, compounded quarterly; this is equivalent to 3% interest each quarter. The 12% rate in this example is sometimes referred to as the *stated interest rate*, the *quoted rate*, or the *nominal rate*. However, when interest is compounded more than once a year, the actual rate the depositor receives is greater than the quoted rate. The true rate is often called the *effective annual interest rate* or the *effective annual yield*.

Calculating and Comparing Effective Annual Rates (p. 46) In general, the relationship between the quoted interest rate and the effective annual rate (EAR) is as follows:

$$EAR = (1 + q/m)^m - 1$$

where m is the number of times per year interest is compounded and q is the quoted interest rate. In the context of present and future values, the formula for compounding m times per year over t years is

$$FV = PV \times (1 + r/m)^{mt}.$$

EARs and APRs (p. 48) We define EAR as the interest rate expressed as if it were compounded once a year. The *APR* or *annual percentage rate* is defined as the interest rate charged per period multiplied by the number of periods per year. Thus, for monthly compounding, the relationship between EAR and APR is as follows:

$$EAR = (1 + APR/12)^{12} - 1.$$

IV. LOAN TYPES AND LOAN AMORTIZATION (p. 50)

The three basic forms of loans are: pure-discount loans, interest-only loans, and amortized loans. Below we discuss the application of present value principles to these three kinds of loans.

Pure Discount Loans (p. 50) A *pure-discount loan* is a loan which is repaid in a single payment; the single payment therefore represents principal plus interest for the period of the loan. The mathematics of pure-discount loans is simply the mathematics of single cash flows.

Interest-Only Loans (p. 51) *Interest-only loans* require payment of interest each year and repayment of the principal at a later date.

Amortized Loans (p. 51) An *amortized loan* requires that the lender make periodic payments which include interest plus repayment of a portion of the principal. A table showing which describes the periodic payments, as well as the interest and principal portion of each payment, is called an *amortization schedule*.

KEY TERMS AND CONCEPTS

Annual percentage rate (APR) - interest rate per period times number of periods per year. (p. 48)
Annuity - a level stream of cash flows for a fixed period of time. (p. 37)
Annuity due - an annuity for which the cash flows occur at the beginning of the period. (p. 43)
Consol - a type of perpetuity. (p. 43)
Discount rate - the rate used to calculate the present value of future cash flows. (p. 32)
Effective annual rate (EAR) - the interest rate expressed as if compounded annually (p. 46)
Perpetuity - an annuity in which the cash flows continue forever. (p. 43)
Stated interest rate - the interest rate expressed in terms of the interest payment each period. Also *quoted interest rate* or *nominal rate*. (p. 46)

CONCEPT TEST

1. A FV with multiple cash flows can be computed by finding the _____ of each deposit and then summing the separate _____. A PV with multiple cash flows can be calculated by separately computing the _____ of each cash flow and then summing the separate _____. (p. 28)

2. An annuity is a series of _____ cash flows that occur at _____ intervals for a _____ number of periods. When the payments occur at the end of the time period, the annuity is referred to as an _____ annuity or a _____ annuity. If payments are at the beginning of the time period, we call the annuity an _____ . (p. 36)

3. The present value of an annuity formula is: PV = _____ , where PV is the present value of the annuity, C is the _____, and PVIFA(r,t) is the _____. PVIFA(r,t) can be determined either from a table or from the following formula: PVIFA(r,t) = _____ . (p. 37)

4. The future value of an annuity formula is: FV = _____ where FV is the future value of the annuity, C is the _____, and FVIFA(r,t) is the _____. FVIFA(r,t) can be determined either from a table or from the following formula: FVIFA(r,t) = _____ . (p. 42)

5. A perpetuity is a perpetual series of _____ cash flows, occurring at _____ intervals. The PV of a perpetuity formula is: PV = _____ . The formula can also be solved for C, and written as: C = _____ . It can also be solved for r: r = _____ . (p. 43)

6. A quoted interest rate is also called a _____ interest rate or a _____ interest rate. When interest is compounded more than once a year, the actual interest rate is _____ than the quoted interest rate. The actual interest rate is often called the effective annual interest rate or _____. The effective annual rate (EAR) is computed as follows: EAR = _____ where m is the number of times per year interest is compounded and q is the quoted interest rate. When interest is compounded m times per year, the future value equals _____ . (p. 46)

7. The three basic forms of loans are: pure-discount loans, interest-only loans, and amortized loans. A pure-discount loan is a loan which is repaid in a_____ which includes _____ plus _____ for the loan period. Interest-only loans require payment of _____ each year, and repayment of _____ later. An amortized loan requires that the lender make periodic payments that include _____ plus repayment of a portion of the _____ . Two common forms of amortized loans are: a loan payment schedule which requires periodic repayment of a fixed portion of the _____ plus _____ ; and, a loan payment which is constant over the life of the loan, so that successive payments repay progressively _____ portions of the principal and correspondingly _____ interest payments. (p. 50)

ANSWERS TO CONCEPT TEST

1. future value; future values; present value; present values
2. equal; regular; fixed; ordinary; regular; annuity due
3. $C \times PVIFA(r,t)$; constant payment; present value interest factor for an annuity; $(1 - 1/(1+r)^t)/r$
4. $C \times FVIFA(r,t)$; constant payment; future value interest factor for an annuity; $((1+r)^t - 1)/r$
5. equal; regular; (C/r); $(PV \times r)$; (C/PV)
6. stated; nominal; greater; effective annual yield; $[1+(q/m)^m] - 1$; $PV \times [1+(r/m)]^{mt}$
7. single payment; interest; principal; interest; principal; interest; principal; larger; smaller

PROBLEMS

1. Compute the present values of the following ordinary annuities:

Payment	Years	Interest rate	Present Value
$678.09	7	13%	
$7,968.26	13	6%	
$20,322.93	23	4%	
$69,712.54	4	31%	

2. Compute the future values of the following ordinary annuities:

Payment	Years	Interest rate	Future Value
$123	13	13%	
$4,555	8	8%	
$74,484	5	10%	
$167,332	9	1%	

3. A local bank is offering 9% interest, compounded monthly, on savings accounts. If you deposit $700 today, how much will you have in 2 years? How much will you have in 2.5 years?

4. For each of the following, calculate the effective annual rate (EAR):

Stated rate	Number of times compounded	Effective rate
5%	semiannually	
11%	quarterly	
16%	daily	

5. You have just joined the investment banking firm of Knot, Wirthem, et al. They have offered you two different salary arrangements. You can have $50,000 per year for the next 3 years or $25,000 per year for the next 3 years, along with a $50,000 signing bonus today. If the market interest rate is 16%, which salary arrangement do you prefer?

6. A bank pays interest compounded monthly; the EAR is 8%. What is the quoted rate?

7. A local loan shark offers 'four for five on payday,' this means you borrow $4 today and you must repay $5 in 6 days, when you get your paycheck. What is the effective annual interest rate for this loan?

8. You expect to receive an annuity of $1000 per year for the next five years. The market rate of interest is 12%. Assuming that you do not spend any of the income at any other time, what is the most you can spend from these payments at the end of five years? What is the most you can spend today?

9. An investment will increase in value by 270% over the next 17 years. What is the annual interest rate which, when compounded quarterly, provides this return?

10. Consider a perpetuity that pays $100 per year; the market rate of interest is 10%. What is the PV of the perpetuity? What is the PV of the perpetuity three years from now? What is the present value of the perpetuity n years from now? Under what circumstances does the value of a perpetuity change?

11. A firm invests $3 million in a project which will yield a perpetuity of $1 million per year. What is the discount rate r for which this project's present value is $4.5 million?

CHAPTER 8

NET PRESENT VALUE AND OTHER INVESTMENT CRITERIA

CONCEPTS FOR REVIEW

This chapter extends our discussion of valuation techniques to nonfinancial assets. Although some new terminology is introduced, the underlying idea remains: good managers will invest only in those assets that will increase the value of the firm and, therefore, the current market price of its common stock.

CHAPTER HIGHLIGHTS

In this chapter we examine five of the most commonly used criteria for making capital budgeting decisions: (1) net present value, (2) payback period, (3) average accounting return, (4) internal rate of return, and (5) the profitability index. Our major conclusion is that the net present value rule is generally the most appropriate criterion for capital budgeting decisions.

I. NET PRESENT VALUE (p. 70)

The net present value concept is of primary concern to decision-makers because it results in capital budgeting decisions that maximize the current price of the firm's common stock.

The Basic Idea (p. 70) An investment is "good" if it creates value for its owners. The net present value (NPV) approach measures *how much* value a given investment creates. Consider the following:

Example Suppose you are considering the formation of a corporation with a one-year life. It is being formed in order to acquire an asset which costs $200,000 and which, you are certain, can be sold one year from now for $250,000. You would like to convince each of 100 investors (including yourself) to purchase a share in this corporation for $2000. Since each investor is a 1% owner, each investor would then receive 1% of $250,000, or $2500, one year from now. Assume the market rate of interest is 8%. Is this investment opportunity attractive to potential investors?

If the corporation purchases this asset today, the present value of $250,000 to be received next year is $250,000/1.08 = $231,481.48. In well-functioning financial markets, investors would be willing to pay as much as $231,481.48 to receive $250,000 in one year. Since the cost of the asset is $200,000, the difference between the asset's current market value and its cost is $231,481.48 – 200,000 = $31,481.48. This difference is the **Net Present Value (NPV)**.

Since the firm consists of one asset, this present value is the value of the corporation once the asset is purchased. An investor who purchases one share for $2,000 and then wishes to immediately sell his 1% share in the financial market will be able to sell it for $2,314.81 (= .01 × $231,481.48).

Further, the NPV of an investor's share is $314.81. This is 1% of the NPV of the firm (i.e., 1% of the difference between $231,481.48 and $200,000), or as the difference between the present value of one share ($2,314.81) and the cost of one share ($2,000). So, an investor who chooses to sell his share immediately will realize a net gain equal to 1% of the NPV of the corporation.

The above example illustrates several points. First, an investment with a positive NPV provides a net benefit to investors equal to the NPV; thus, an investment with a negative NPV should be rejected. Second, the NPV not only provides a criterion for determining whether an investment is acceptable, but is also an unambiguous measure of the value of the investment. Third, a corporate investment with a positive NPV provides a net benefit to the shareholder equal to his proportionate share of the NPV of the corporate investment. Fourth, the management of the firm can determine whether an investment is acceptable to the stockholders without regard for the preferences of individual stockholders; i.e., the NPV is the net gain to the stockholder, regardless of whether he intends to keep his share or to sell it immediately. Finally, the results suggest the **NPV rule: Management should accept investments with positive NPVs since such investments provide value to the stockholders, and they must reject investments with negative NPVs because such investments destroy stockholder value.**

Estimating Net Present Value (p. 71) The formula for computing the NPV of an investment is:

$$NPV = -C_0 + C_1/(1+r)^1 + C_2/(1+r)^2 + \ldots C_t/(1+r)^t$$

where t represents the last period during which a payment is received, C_0 is the initial outlay, C_1 is the payment one year from now, and r is the appropriate discount rate.

II. THE PAYBACK RULE (p. 74)

The **payback period** is the time required to recover the initial investment for a capital budgeting project from the subsequent cash inflows produced by the project. Unfortunately, it has several major deficiencies that render it inadequate for use as the sole criterion by which a capital budgeting decision will be made.

Defining the Rule (p. 74) The **payback period rule** specifies that an investment is acceptable if the sum of its cash flows equals the initial investment before some specified cutoff time period.

Learning Tip: Many students (and businesspeople) advocate the use of the payback period because it is easy to calculate. But is this a good reason to use it? No! Consider the list below . . .

Analyzing the Rule (p. 76) Deficiencies of the payback rule include:

1. The timing of cash flows within the payback period is ignored, thereby treating these cash flows as equally valuable; in contrast, the net present value properly discounts these cash flows.
2. All cash flows after the cutoff date are ignored, while the NPV discounts all cash flows.
3. There is no objective criterion for choosing an optimal cutoff time period.

Redeeming Qualities of the Rule (p. 77)

1. It is quickly and easily applied; thus, it is appropriate for frequent, small-scale decisions that don't warrant extensive analysis.
2. It is biased toward liquidity.
3. It (crudely) adjusts for risk in later cash flows (by ignoring them).

III. THE AVERAGE ACCOUNTING RETURN (p. 78)

The **average accounting return (AAR)** equals the average net income of an investment divided by its average book value. The **average accounting return rule** specifies that an investment is acceptable if its average accounting return exceeds a specified target level of return.

Learning Tip: Since the AAR is just net income divided by book value of assets, it is the project-level analog to the ROA measure calculated for the firm from Chapter 3.

The AAR rule has several serious deficiencies. First, it uses accounting income and book value data, which generally are not closely related to cash flows, the relevant data for financial decision-making. Second, it ignores the time value of money. And third, the target AAR must be arbitrarily specified because it is not a rate of return in the financial market sense.

IV. THE INTERNAL RATE OF RETURN (p. 80)

The **internal rate of return (IRR)** is the rate of return (or discount rate) which equates the PV of the cash inflows with the cash cost of the investment; alternatively, the IRR is defined as the rate of return for an investment. Algebraically, IRR is the solution for the discount rate r in the following equation:

$$C_0 = C_1/(1+r) + C_2/(1+r)^2 + \ldots C_t/(1+r)^t$$

where C_i is the cash flow for year i. The right side of the above equation is the present value of all cash inflows expected for the project under consideration; C_t is the cash inflow expected at the end of year t, which is the last year that cash inflows are expected from the project.

Learning Tip: *Solving this equation for r is equivalent to solving for the yield to maturity of a level coupon bond, as discussed in Chapter 6. Therefore, the value of r can be determined by either trial-and-error or with a financial calculator. For either approach, the solution technique is analogous to the corresponding solution of the yield to maturity problem presented previously.*

The IRR can also be interpreted as the annually compounded rate of return on the initial outlay (assuming we are using annual time periods). Hence the IRR decision rule: **An investment project is <u>acceptable</u> if the IRR is greater than the rate of return which could be earned in the financial markets on investments of equal risk; an investment project is <u>unacceptable</u> if the IRR is less than the relevant rate of return in the financial markets.**

The relationship between discount rates, NPVs, and IRRs is apparent in the **NPV profile**, a graph of an investment's possible NPVs computed using several discount rates. NPV profiles have the following characteristics:

1. As the discount rate increases, the NPV decreases; i.e., NPV and r are inversely related.
2. The slope of the NPV profile is an indication of the sensitivity of the investment's NPV to the discount rate - the steeper the slope, the more sensitive the NPV.
3. The IRR is the point where the NPV profile intersects the X-axis (i.e., where NPV = 0).

Problems with the IRR (p. 83) Problems arise in applying the internal rate of return criterion occur when we have nonconventional cash flows and/or mutually exclusive investments. A **conventional** cash flow pattern consists of a cash outlay followed by a series of inflows. A **nonconventional** series of cash flows includes more than one net outflow. The latter may result in the existence of more than one rate that equates the PV of the inflows and the PV of the outlays; i.e., **multiple IRRs**. Since there is no basis for choosing either rate as the relevant IRR, it is impossible to apply the IRR criterion when cash flows change sign more than once.

An **independent investment project** is one for which acceptance or rejection does not affect, and is not affected by, the acceptance or rejection of any other projects. **Mutually exclusive investment projects** are those projects for which acceptance of any one project implies the rejection of another.

Learning Tip: *Independent projects can be evaluated on a "stand-alone" basis. Mutually exclusive projects, on the other hand, must be evaluated simultaneously. Not doing so exposes one to the risk of accepting a good project but foregoing the ability to accept its better substitute later.*

The difficulties encountered in applying the IRR criterion to mutually exclusive projects arise when the projects being compared differ with respect to either scale or timing. In the former case, there are differences in the size of the initial outlay for the projects under consideration; in the latter case, the differences are generally between one project whose cash flows are concentrated in the early years of the project's life and another project whose cash flows are concentrated in the later years. In either case, it is possible that the NPV of one project is higher than that of its mutually exclusive substitute, while its IRR is lower. In this case, we return to our primary goal: maximize firm value, which suggests that, all else equal, we should select the project with the highest NPV.

Redeeming Qualities of the IRR (p. 87) The IRR is popular because it describes project profitability in terms of rates, rather than dollars, which makes communication and comparisons easier. Further, since it is related to the NPV technique, it often leads to the same "Invest/Don't invest" decision as the NPV rule for a given project.

V. THE PROFITABILITY INDEX (p. 88)

The **profitability index (PI)** equals the PV of the future cash flows divided by the initial investment. If this ratio exceeds 1.0, the project's NPV exceeds zero, and the investment is desirable.

The PI is useful when a firm is subject to **capital rationing** during the current time period. Capital rationing occurs when, for whatever reason, the amount of investable funds is limited and a firm has more positive NPV projects than can currently be undertaken. The proposed solution is to rank the projects by profitability index, and accept those with the highest values. This will, in most circumstances, result in the maximum total increase in firm value.

VI. THE PRACTICE OF CAPITAL BUDGETING (p. 89)

In surveys of large corporations, discounted cash flow (DCF) approaches such as NPV, IRR, and PI, are the most commonly used capital budgeting techniques. It appears that 80% or more use discounted cash flow, but not necessarily to the exclusion of other procedures.

KEY TERMS AND CONCEPTS

Average accounting return - investment's average net income divided by average book value. (p. 78)

Discounted cash flow valuation - valuing an investment by discounting its future cash flows. (p. 71)

Internal rate of return - the discount rate that makes the NPV of an investment zero. (p. 80)

Multiple rates of return - possibility that more than one discount rate makes the NPV of an investment zero. (p. 85)

Mutually exclusive investment decisions - situation where taking one investment prevents the taking of another. (p. 85)

Net present value - the difference between an investment's market value and its cost. (p. 71)

Net present value profile - graphical representation of the relationship between an investment's NPVs and various discount rates. (p. 82)

Payback period - time required for an investment's cash flows to equal its initial cost. (p. 74)

Profitability index - present value of an investment's future cash flows divided by its cost. (p. 88)

CONCEPT TEST

1. PV analysis of an investment specifies that it is _____ if the PV of the future cash inflows is _____ the cash outlay; the investment is _____ if the PV of future cash inflows is _____ the cash outlay. (p. 70)

2. The NPV of an asset equals the difference between the PV of the future _____ produced by the asset and the _____ of the asset. An investment is acceptable if its NPV is _____ . An investment is unacceptable if its NPV is _____ . The NPV of an asset measures the _____ which accrues to the _____ of the firm if the asset is acquired. Thus, the use of the NPV criterion is consistent with the financial manager's goal of maximizing the _____ of the firm's common stock. (p. 71)

3. The payback period is the amount of time required to recover the _____ for a capital budgeting project from the future _____ produced by the project. The payback period rule specifies that an investment is _____ if the payback period is less than a specified _____ . Deficiencies of the rule include: the _____ of cash flows within the payback period is ignored, thereby treating these cash flows as _____ ; all cash flows after the _____ are ignored; and, there is no objective criterion for choosing the optimal _____ . The primary advantage of the payback rule is its _____ . (p. 74)

4. The average accounting return for an investment project equals _____ attributed to the asset divided by _____ of the asset. The AAR rule specifies that an investment is _____ if its average accounting return exceeds a _____ . Deficiencies of the AAR are: the method uses _____ income and _____ value data, rather than _____ ; the AAR ignores the _____ ; and, the _____ must be arbitrarily specified. (p. 78)

5. The IRR is the rate of return (or discount rate) which equates the _____ of the future _____ for an investment with its _____ . The IRR is the rate of return which equates the NPV of an investment to _____ . An investment is _____ if the IRR exceeds the rate of return that could be earned in the financial markets on investments of equal risk; an investment project is _____ if the IRR is less than the relevant rate of return in the financial markets. (p. 80)

6. The IRR criterion may not correctly indicate whether an investment is acceptable. The problems which arise in applying the IRR criterion are associated with the following situations: _____ cash flows and _____ investments. (p. 83)

7. A "conventional" cash flow for a capital budgeting project has a _____ cash flow followed by _____ cash flows. A _____ series of cash flows changes sign more than once, and may have more than one IRR. (p. 85)

8. An _____ investment project is an investment whose acceptance or rejection does not affect, and is not affected by, the acceptance or rejection of any other projects. A mutually exclusive project is a project for which acceptance implies _____ of another. The difficulties encountered in applying the IRR criterion to mutually exclusive projects arise when the projects being compared differ with respect to either _____ or _____. Incorrect decisions are avoided by: (1) applying the _____ criterion; or, (2) applying the IRR criterion to the _____ cash flows. (p. 85)

9. The profitability index is the _____ of the future _____ divided by _____. If the PI exceeds _____, the investment is _____, because the PV of the future cash inflows exceeds the _____. Any _____ investment acceptable by the PI criterion is also acceptable by the NPV criterion. Problems may arise in applying the PI to _____ investment projects. Incorrect decisions are avoided by: (1) applying the _____ criterion; (2) applying the criterion to the _____ cash flows. (p. 88)

ANSWERS TO CONCEPT TEST

1. acceptable; greater than; unacceptable; less than
2. cash inflows; cost; positive; negative; value; owners; price
3. initial investment; cash inflows; acceptable; cutoff time period; timing; equally valuable; cutoff time period; cutoff time period; simplicity
4. average net income; average book value; acceptable; specified target level; accounting; book; cash flows; time value of money; target AAR
5. present value; cash inflows; cost; zero; acceptable; unacceptable
6. nonconventional; mutually exclusive
7. negative; positive; nonconventional;
8. independent; rejection; scale; timing; net present value; incremental
9. present value; cash inflows; initial investment; one; acceptable; initial investment; independent; mutually exclusive; net present value; incremental

PROBLEMS

For Problems 1-6, use the following cash flows for projects A and B:

A: (-$2000, $500, $600, $700, $800)
B: (-$2000, $950, $850, $400, $300)

1. Calculate the payback period for projects A and B.

2. Calculate the internal rate of return for projects A and B.

3. If A and B are mutually exclusive and the required rate of return is 5%, which should be accepted?

4. If the discount rate is 12%, and A and B are mutually exclusive, which project should be accepted?

5. At what discount rate will we be indifferent between A and B?

6. Compute the IRR for investments with the following cash flows in years 0, 1 and 2: (-$60, $155, -$100) and ($60, -$155, $100). How do you interpret the results in terms of the IRR criterion?

7. You have been asked to analyze an investment with the following cash flows in years 0, 1 and 2, respectively: (-$51, $100, -$50). Compute the IRR. Is the investment acceptable? The required return is unknown.

8. Consider the following abbreviated financial statements for a proposed investment:

Year	0	1	2	3	4
Gross Book Value	$160	$160	$160	$160	$160
Accumulated Dep.		40	80	120	160
Net Book Value	$160	$120	$80	$40	$0
Sales		$95	$90	$97	$80
Costs		33	30	25	10
Depreciation		40	40	40	40
Taxes (50%)		$11	$10	$16	$15
Net Income		$11	$10	$16	$15

What is the average accounting return (AAR) for the proposed investment?

9. What is the internal rate of return for the investment described in the previous problem?

10. Calculate the IRR of an investment with cash flows in years 0, 1 and 2: ($792, -$1780, $1000).

11. For the investment identified in the previous problem, determine the acceptability of the investment when the required return is 10%; when it is 12%; and when it is 14%.

12. You can borrow $8000, to be repaid in installments of $2,200 at the end of each of the next 5 years. Use the IRR to determine whether this loan is preferable to borrowing at the rate of 11.5%.

13. A firm is considering the following mutually exclusive investment projects. Project A requires an initial outlay of $500 and will return $120 per year for the next seven years. Project B requires an initial outlay of $5,000 and will return $1,350 per year for the next five years. The required rate of return is 10%. Use the net present value criterion to determine which investment is preferable.

14. Calculate the internal rate of return for each of the projects described in the previous problem.

15. Calculate the profitability index for each of the investments described in the previous problem.

r